Abuse of Child and Childhood

(The Case of Kerala)

N.V. Raveendran

ATLANTIC

PUBLISHERS & DISTRIBUTORS (P) LTD

Published by

ATLANTIC

PUBLISHERS & DISTRIBUTORS (P) LTD

7/22, Ansari Road, Darya Ganj, New Delhi-110002
Phones : +91-11-40775252, 23273880, 23275880, 23280451
Fax : +91-11-23285873
Web : www.atlanticbooks.com
E-mail : orders@atlanticbooks.com

Branch Office
5, Nallathambi Street, Wallajah Road, Chennai-600002
Phones : +91-44-64611085, 32413319
E-mail : chennai@atlanticbooks.com

ISBN 978-81-269-1859-1

Printed in India at Nice Printing Press, A-33/3A, Site-IV, Industrial Area, Sahibabad, Ghaziabad, U.P.

Preface

Geographically, Kerala is only 1.2 per cent of the Indian Union. The child population of the state is 2.37 per cent of the national total. In literacy rate the state is the highest in the Union and in infant mortality rate, the lowest. Kerala's economic progress is above national average and the state's human development index is higher than that of most developed countries. The problems the children of Kerala faced at the time of preparing this report were in a number of ways different from those of the children in other parts of the country. The familial and social atmosphere of any state has to be safe and strong enough to shape the lives of its future citizens. With all its plus points, whether Kerala maintains such an atmosphere might be an issue for any sensitive citizen in the state.

Child abuse is a global phenomenon. Why the problem did not bother the society of Kerala till recently has socio-cultural and ethical explanations. In societies like the Western where there are deviant approaches to child rearing, this has been a problem for quite some time. They have stringent law enforcement mechanisms to check child abuse. A study on child abuse in India by the Ministry of Women and Child Development (2007) exposed a situation which was far from comfortable for the children in India. This has been a sure motivation to ponder over the situation of children in the state of Kerala.

The state of Kerala has legally brought into being all measures adopted by the Central Government towards ensuring safety and protection of the children. Yet the problems of the children in the state are becoming increasingly complex, demanding detailed examination of the causes.

This study is based on the data collected from three regions of the state—south, centre and north. Familial, social, ethical and economic aspects were focused during data collection. The early chapters, however, discuss the theoretical aspects in a wider perspective.

During the tenure of the study, I met many individuals who could look into the present state of childhood in India in general and Kerala in particular and speak out their views. The children of the state have lost the security of the joint family system. This is not to suggest that this is not happening to children elsewhere in the country. Communal responsibility too has disappeared. Tender relations have degenerated into extremely selfish ways of looking at life. The visual media has let loose wanton images of life full of pleasure hunts and other temptations that pull the young and the old alike towards a life devoid of compassion, tolerance and patience. The state had a system of child rearing which although with several ills, was based on indigenous culture. This child-friendly and compassionate perception has given way to suspicion—the adults in general suspect the child's innocence and the child has no trust in the adult. Erosion of values hitherto considered eternal is eating up the social fabric of the state.

The picture presented by a study like this may not be a pleasing one. Yet it cannot be said that things are beyond recovery. But if the current mindset of the populace towards life as such continues, the consequence is predictable—there will be social disarray in the state which would be detrimental to the growth of children on whose shoulders rest the future of the nation.

In this study, perspective is not a social scientist's, but that of a person who is concerned about the problem. The constraints of research work in social science haven't affected the quality and range of this attempt. Since a methodology suitable to the present work has been adopted, in this study, statistical analysis of data is minimal. Some definitions and explanations are repeated at various places to provide clarity.

Although the study is based on the findings in the state of Kerala, the issues and concerns it brings to light are universal in nature and applicable to all the states of India. It will provide a scientific basis for understanding the following:

- The family and community factors which increase the rise of child abuse.
- The differential consequences of child abuse depending upon its duration and severity.
- The factors that increase the possibility of positive child outcomes despite maltreatment or abuse.
- The impact of various societal innervations like child welfare programmes, foster care and mental health services.

The book will be useful for policymakers, planners, social workers, NGOs and those concerned with checking child abuse in India and mitigating its effects.

N.V. Raveendran

Acknowledgements

I gratefully acknowledge the support received from the University Grants Commission without which the study would not have been possible. I am thankful to the Principal, NSS Hindu College, Changanacherry, and Professors K.R. Narayanan, K. Viyayan and T.K. Levan for all they have done in furtherance of the study.

N.V. Raveendran

Contents

Introduction

1

Child abuse, an unfortunate aspect of childhood, is a global phenomenon. After the Second World War Europeans and Americans have conducted in-depth studies on the incidents in a child's life that deter its growth into a self-respecting adult. In India a conscious attempt to assess the problems of the child was made only recently. Outcome—the Government is aware of the existence of the problem. There are non-governmental agencies as well who try to intervene when situation demands. The problem, however, is larger than it appears to be. The changes in the socio-economic environment have added to the complexity of the Indian child's plight. The mode of life, hitherto considered worthy, has a rupture. This is pointed out by many as a significant mark of change.

Childhood in India faces problems that need great attention, because these problems are capable of causing serious damage to the children who should sustain a healthy society. It goes without saying that any impairment to childhood will cause serious harm to the nation. The state of Kerala too has enough reasons to be concerned about its children.

Defining child abuse is a complex issue. Since this is an area where not much research has been done in India, especially in Kerala, and since this is an 'emergent' issue, the magnitude of which is yet to be gauged, which is related to the issues specific to each region and even to each community, definitions can vary. That means different definitions are possible. Moreover, the way law authorities and NGOs look at the problem even at the same place differ, as their perspectives and concerns are different. Looking at the problem from a wider perspective may give a better idea which may help reach a definition.

Child and Childhood

The historical accounts of family life that relates the social conception of 'child' and 'childhood' relevant to this study could be located in the European treatises of the middle ages that "use a terminology which strikes us as purely verbal: childhood, puerility, adolescence, youth, senility, old age—each age signifying a different period of life" (Aries 1962: 18-19). The medieval text *Le Grand Proprietaire* deals with the ages of man corresponding to the number of planets—there are seven of them. The first is childhood which lasts until the seventh year. The next stage is called *pueritia* which lasts till fourteen. The third age is called adolescence which according to Constantine ends in the twenty-first year. According to Isidore it lasts till 28 or may go up to 45. Youth comes only next which occupies the central position and ends at 45 or 50. Then follows *senectitude* which is half way between youth and old age. The next is old age which ends with death (Aries, 1962:22).

A thirteenth century poem that expounds the ages of man has an insightful comment on childhood:

> The child six summers old
> Is not worth much when all is told
> But one must take every care
> To see that he is fed good care
> For he who does not start life well
> Will finish badly, one can tell. (Aries 22)

Childhood was considered "not worth much"—a child is a 'small adult'—in the middle ages. Therefore, in the west, looking at "childhood" as a distinctive phenomenon is a modern attitude. But the seventeenth century European attitude differs by drawing it as a period of innocence and simplicity on the one hand and of ignorance and weakness on the other. A prayer by Jacqueline Pascal goes thus: "Grant, O. Lord, that we may always be children in our simplicity and innocence, as *people of the world are always children in their ignorance and weakness*" (Aries 23). Although in the medieval European society the idea of childhood did not exist, this was not to suggest that children were neglected. However, as soon as the child could live without the constant solicitude of his mother, he belonged to the adult society.

The construction of the idea of childhood has been linked to the establishment of formal education in the nineteenth century and the construction of the idea of adolescence originates in the seventeenth century and took hold as capitalism developed (Wise, J.M. 2008: 55). Within the present day Western society itself the attitude to children vary—"some expect infants to learn independence, some carry children strapped to their bodies for years. Some send them to factories to work. Some expect them to inhabit a world of innocence and play." Youth is a probationary period where one becomes an adolescent (literally meaning becoming adult) or teenager (Wise 55).

At the turn of 20th century children had become emotionally "priceless" in the American culture (Zelizer, V.A. 1985). Children's Bureau was established thereafter to address to the problems of children. Over the years, humane reaction to this attitude led to the current conception of child abuse in the United States. In the sixties, Henry Kempe and his associates provided scientific clue to child maltreatment and described their finding with the term "battered child syndrome" (Kempe, C.H. *et al.* 1962:17-24). Later sexual and emotional maltreatment of children by parents and caretakers were added to the term child abuse (Bourne R. 1979). Before switching over to the discussion of the problem within the social framework of the society of Kerala, it would be worthwhile to look at child abuse from different perspectives and position the problem in the larger global context.

Child Abuse in Europe and America: Definitions in Vogue

Kempe and Gardner (1978) and Gray (1982), while attempting to define child abuse maintain that if a child is injured in his own environment, which is clinically evident, by other individuals who are physically and mentally capable of injuring him, they are said to be abusing the child. Korbin Jill (1981) is a little more descriptive and clear when he says that when a child is physically and mentally tortured, discriminated against others, and deprived of what is due to him, he is clearly an abused child.

Different forms of child abuse include constant scolding, use of unpleasant or threatening words, threats of physical torture, severe physical punishments although this may not require medical attention.

Child abuse is generally categorized as physical, emotional and sexual (neglect also is abuse). Compelling to do hard work, forcing into physical labour, having to do work without protection, come under physical abuse.

The indicators of physical abuse are in most cases visible. Physical weakness caused by insufficient food, or lack of medical attention is an indicator of neglect. Wounds and abrasive skin indicate physical abuse. The British department of health (1988) has listed the following indicators of child abuse:

Physical abuse

Minor injuries

Serious injuries resulting in fracture or head injuries

Premeditated/sadistic injury

Burns and scalds

Repeated abuse resulting from lack of control.

Punishment with implements

Genital/anal area injuries

Shaking

Poisoning

Neglect

Abandonment or desertion

Leaving alone

Malnourishment, lack of food, inappropriate food, or erratic feeding

Lack of warmth

Lack of adequate clothing

Unhygienic home conditions

Lack of protection or exposure to dangers, including moral danger, or lack of supervision appropriate to child's age.

Persistent failure to attend school

Non-organic failure to thrive.

Neglect implies the failure to provide shelter, medical care, education or supervision. Indicators of neglect are scaly and dirty skin, matty and sparse hair, sunken eyes, an aged face, and look particularly apathetic, sad, and anxious. This form of abuse is felt to be the most common form of child maltreatment reported. The "failure to thrive syndrome" has been associated with child neglect. The victims show slow neurological and psychological development (Cantwell, A.B. 1980).

Emotional abuse

Rejection

Lack of praise or encouragement

Lack of comfort and love

Lack of attachment

Lack of stimulation to play

Lack of continuity of care (frequent moves)

Lack of appropriate handling (age-inappropriate expectations)

Serious over protectiveness

Inappropriate nonphysical punishment (locking in bedrooms)

Consistent verbal harassment, criticism, belittlement, withdrawal, denial and rejection are practised in families with parent of abusive nature. It is the "willful destruction or significant impairment of the child's competence". Emotional injuries may be more disabling than some physical injuries and inflict just as much damage on the developing personality. Reporting and intervention are most difficult in the case of emotional abuse [Garbarino, J. and Gilliam, G. (1980)].

Sexual abuse

Inappropriate fondling

Mutual masturbation

Digital penetration

Oral/genital contact

Anal or vaginal intercourse

Exploitation for pornography

Exposure to pornography

Child sexual abuse as a research topic was first introduced by Sigmond Freud in his 1896 paper entitled "The Aetiology of Hysteria", "hysteria" as defined by Freud is known today as neurosis. Using a sample of 18 patients—male and female—from his practice, he concluded that all of them had been the victims of unwanted sexual assaults by various caretakers. The cause of the patient's distress lay in a trauma inflicted by an actor in the child's social environment. The source of internal psychic pain lay in an act inflicted upon the child from outside. This led to his well known 'seduction theory'.

This theory held that hysteria and obsessional neurosis are caused by repressed memories of infantile sexual abuse. Infantile sexual abuse, the root of all neurosis, is premature introduction of sexuality into the experience of the child. The adult who had a normal, non traumatic childhood is able to contain and assimilate sexual feelings into a continuous sense of self. Freud proposed that adults who experienced sexual abuse as a child suffer from unconscious memories and feelings incompatible with the central mass of thoughts and feelings that constitute his or her experience. Psychic disorders are a direct consequence of experiences that cannot be assimilated (Wikipedia).

The most disturbing form of abuse in the economically developed Western Europe is child sexual abuse. Child sexual abuse and exploitation are significant problems in Europe today and it is estimated that between 10 per cent and 20 per cent of children are sexually assaulted during their childhood. There are many forms of abuse including incest, prostitution, pornography, date rape, peer sexual violence and institutional sexual abuse—all are considered abnormal sexual behaviour. Since the 1996 Stockholm World Congress considerable progress has been made in developing measures to combat sexual abuse and exploitation of children but there is still a long way to go, particularly because the crime usually happens in private and victims are often threatened or sworn to secrecy.

Societies like the Canadian, which are in essence European, have legislations that include the idea that families are responsible for the care, supervision and protection of their children; that children have rights that must be protected; that governments are responsible for protecting children from harm; that the best interest of the child is a guiding decision principle (Karen J. Swift 1997:40).

Observable injuries which are non-accidental seen on a child are a sign of physical abuse. However, Canada's criminal code includes a clause providing that teachers, parents, and guardians are justified in using force by way of correction toward a pupil or child if correction does not exceed what is reasonable under the circumstances (Karen 1997:43).

Traditional forms of child neglect outlined in most Western and American legislations include abandonment, children found in unfit or improper circumstances, failure of caretakers to provide necessities, lack of supervision and guidance, delinquent behaviour by the child, denial of medical care, and failure to send a child to school (Karen 1997: 43). Child neglect is comparatively non-controversial and less dramatic than sexual or physical abuse. Distinguishing between poverty, neglect and criminal negligence is a problem.

Emotional and psychological abuse have been recognized in European and American/Canadian legislations for many years, but have been considered difficult to define and prove. Emotional neglect, psychological abuse, and emotional maltreatment are derivative expressions which are not truly synonymous, and have added to the difficulty. A common definition of emotional harm is "demonstrated by anxiety, depression, withdrawal, or self-destructive behaviour" (Karen 44). In fact, any act or attitude that endangers the emotional and mental development of the child is emotional abuse.

Freud's later theories describing children as unreliable witnesses influenced the western approach to child sexual abuse until the late 1970s. To Freud, report by a child on sexual abuse was a fantasy (Masson, J. 1984). In 1984 Government of Canada published the Badgley Report which found that half of the females and one-third of the males in the sample were victims of unwanted sexual acts in childhood. The abusers were mostly members of the child's own family. These findings brought serious attention to the problem which eventually led to law reforms (Government of Canada, 1984). Sexual abuse has turned out to be the most preferred among the different abuses: Cases involving ritual abuse, large scale sexual abuse on an intergenerational basis, abuse perpetrated by such trusted figures as priests and Christian brothers in children's institutions, child pornography and prostitution as lucrative and flourishing businesses, and charges of sexual abuse in the distant past, followed by the defence of false memory syndrome, keep sexual abuse in the forefront of public attention. This issue more than any other raises the question of whether traditional child welfare's almost exclusive focus on parents remains appropriate. Sexual abuse is also an issue that brings gender into the equation in an inescapable way since the majority of the victims are girls, while nearly all perpetrators are males (Karen 46). (The present study holds that the reverse also can be true for the State of Kerala.)

The definition of child abuse, the way the problem was gauged, and the samples studied determine the conclusions arrived at. CPS (Child Protective Services) of the United States records and initiates action upon reports of child maltreatments. The national incidence study on child abuse used the data from CPS to define six different types of maltreatment—physical, sexual, and emotional abuse and physical, emotional and educational neglect.

However, some researchers are of the opinion that official reports are unreliable because each study is imperfect and the true size and scope of the problem remains unexplored (Pecora, P.J. *et al.* 1992). Schene, P. (1987) finds that for every child reported there are seven abused children who are not reported. In the case of the US it is likely that the number of substantiated cases given in official reporting figures underestimates the number of children abused.

The California Child Abuse Reporting Law identifies categories of abuse in five basic areas:

1. **Sexual abuse, sexual assault, sexual exploitation:** Sexual abuse includes direct acts such as sexual assault and indirect acts such as sexual exploitation of the child and pornographic materials.
2. **Neglect:** Neglect of the child, either "severe" or "general" including acts and omissions resulting in harm or threatening to harm the child's health or welfare. Severe neglect refers to the negligent failure of a person to protect the child from severe malnutrition or medically diagnosed non-organic failure to thrive.
3. **Emotional abuse:** Willful cruelty or unjustified punishment. This section is defined as the direct infliction of or permitting of a child to suffer, unjustifiable physical pain or mental suffering.
4. **Unlawful corporal punishment or injury:** This is defined as any cruel or inhuman corporal punishment or injury resulting in traumatic condition.
5. **Physical abuse:** Physical abuse is seen as injury that is inflicted by other than accidental means on the child (Lawrence 1997).

Nearly five children die every day in America from abuse and neglect. In 2009, an estimated 1,770 children died from abuse in the United States. In the same year, Children's Advocacy Centers around the country served over 254,000 child victims of abuse, providing victim advocacy and support to these children and their families. In 2010, this number was over 266,000.

2009 National Abuse Statistics—USA

- Approximately 702,000 children were victims of maltreatment (unique instances).
- 44 states reported that more than 3 million children received preventative services from Child Protective Services agencies.

- Victims in the age group of birth to 1 year had the highest rate of victimization, at 20.6 per 1,000 children of the same age group in the national population.
- Of the children who experienced maltreatment or abuse, over 75 per cent experienced neglect; more than 15 per cent were physically abused; just under 10 per cent were sexually abused; and just under 10 per cent were psychologically maltreated.
- Nearly 90 per cent of all recorded and duplicate perpetrators of child maltreatment were parents of the victim(s).

Among the over 141,000 children served by Children's Advocacy Centers (3) around the USA from January through June 2011, some startling statistics include:

- 53,932 children were aged 0 to 6 years
- 51,196 children were aged 7 to 12 years
- 36,131 children were aged 13 to 18 years
- 95,120 children reported sexual abuse
- 25,414 children reported physical abuse
- 88,312 children participated in forensic interviewing at a Children's Advocacy Center

Among the over 116,000 alleged offenders investigated for instances of child abuse from January through June 2011, some startling statistics include:

- 75,829 were 18+ years old
- 11,973 were aged 13 to 17 years
- 7,911 were under age 13 years
- 45,496 were a parent or step-parent of the victim
- 23,763 were related to the child victim in another way
- 36,628 were an unrelated person the victim knew

Source: (1) Every Child Matters Education Fund (2009). We Can Do Better: Child Abuse and Neglect Deaths in the U.S. (2) U.S. Department of Health and Human Services: Administration for Children and Families. Child Maltreatment.

(3) National Children's Alliance 2010 national statistics and January through June 2011 national statistics collected from Children's Advocacy Center members.

National Child Abuse Hotline 1-800-4-A-Child (America) reports that over 3 million reports of child abuse are made every year in the United States; however, those reports can include multiple children. In 2007, approximately 5.8 million children were involved in an estimated 3.2 million child abuse reports and allegations. According to this agency,

- A report of child abuse is made every ten seconds.
- Almost five children die everyday as a result of child abuse. More than three out of four are under the age of 4.
- It is estimated that between 60-85 per cent of child fatalities due to maltreatment are not recorded as such on death certificates.
- 90 per cent of child sexual abuse victims know the perpetrator in some way; 68 per cent are abused by family members.
- Child abuse occurs at every socio-economic level, across ethnic and cultural lines, within all religions and at all levels of education.
- 31 per cent of women in prison in the United States were abused as children.
- Over 60 per cent of people in drug rehabilitation centers report being abused or neglected as a child.
- About 30 per cent of abused and neglected children will later abuse their own children, continuing the horrible cycle of abuse.
- About 80 per cent of 21-year-old that were abused as children met criteria for at least one psychological disorder.
- The estimated annual cost of child abuse and neglect in the United States for 2007 is $104 billion.
- Abused children are 25 per cent more likely to experience teen pregnancy.

In the U.K. laws have been enacted to contain abuse of children. The Children Act 1989 focuses on the following themes:

The Child's welfare is the paramount consideration.

Children are generally best looked after in the family and parents should be supported in this act.

The primary target for attention are "children in need", who are those who are unlikely to achieve or maintain a reasonable standard of health or development, or are disabled. Appropriate services should be provided for families with these children including: advice and counseling, social activities, assistance with travel, aid with arranging a holiday, home help, family centres and day care.

Applications can be made to the courts for care or supervision orders for children suffering, or likely to suffer "significant harm", either in terms of ill treatment or impairment of health or development. These can last upto the age of 18 years unless discharged earlier. "Parental responsibility" can be retained by the parents of children living away from home.

According to a legislation by UK Department of Health (1989) children are to be consulted on matters affecting them. (U.K. Department of Health, 1989). To the above legislation there is provision for Emergency Protection Orders which a Magistrate can order legal protection for a child being abused or under threat of abuse up to eight days. Parton (1989:55) observes that self report studies indicate that the extent of physical, sexual, emotional and other forms of abuse far exceeds that which is officially notified and recorded.

The official publication of the British Home Office (1991) *Working together under the Children Act 1989* uses four definitions of abuse:

Neglect: The persistent or severe neglect of a child or failure to protect a child from exposure to any kind of danger, including cold or starvation, or extreme failure to carry out important aspects of care, resulting in the significant impairment of the child's health or development, including non-organic failure to thrive.

Physical Injury: Actual or likely physical injury to a child, or failure to prevent physical injury (or suffering) to a child including deliberate poisoning, suffocation and Munchausen's syndrome by proxy.

Sexual Abuse: Actual or likely sexual exploitation of a child or adolescent. The child may be dependent and/or developmentally immature.

Emotional Abuse: Actual or likely severe adverse effect on the emotional and behavioural development of a child caused by persistent and severe emotional ill-treatment or rejection. All abuse involves some emotional ill-treatment. This category should be used where it is the main or sole form of abuse (U.K. Home Office, 1991:48-49).

In Finland, after 1969, parents did not have a right to inflict even mild forms of corporal punishment on their children. If they assault the child physically the legal system treats the parents as any other abuser. The country is now concerned more about sexual abuse not only in the families but also about the commercial exploitation of children for sexual purposes (Tarja Poso 1997:45-47).

It has been found by Western researchers that some parents and caretakers are capable of inflicting injuries of unimaginable magnitude on their children. The indicators of physical abuse include bruises, welts, lacerations, abdominal injuries, ocular damage, burns, scalds, and bone fractures to death. Shaking an infant may cause injury to the child's neck, bleeding within the skull, and brain injury that may be associated with early death (Caffey, J. 1972). The medical clues to severe child abuse involving injuries to bone and soft tissue are found on physical examination or on X-ray film. The instruments used for maltreatment vary from stick, electric wires, belts and bare hands and feet to boiling water and pokers. In one survey, ninety-five implements of child torture were reported (Johnson, C.F. 1985).

Africa

Recent events demonstrate that the present day African environment denies the average African Child any true joy of living. The African child continues to suffer the effects of war, poverty, ignorance, malnutrition, under-nutrition, starvation, diseases especially AIDS, exploitation, oppression and neglect. The African girl child in particular lives under the constant threat of sexual, physical and emotional abuse.

The recent increases in the different forms of child abuse, exploitation and suffering in Africa is extremely distressing. Under the guise of tradition and poverty, African children continue to be exploited, oppressed and abused by so-called adults whose job it is to protect them.

Although child abuse does not only exist in Africa, it is more prevalent here. Abuse of African children takes many forms. The phenomenon of child trafficking for forced or compulsory labour is growing so fast that most countries in Africa fit into one of the three categories—sending countries, transit countries and receiving countries. Child trafficking has become a very profitable, multi billion dollar business for the organised syndicates involved. As they flee poverty, Africa's children are being increasingly exploited by traffickers, who make billions of dollars a year by buying children for as little as 14 dollars a head and sending them to slavery in Europe or the Gulf.

According to a recent ILO report, an estimated 60 per cent of sex workers in Italy are from Nigeria. In the words of Meera Sethi of the International Immigration Organization, Africa has become a "supplier of fresh flesh" for countries in the European Union, via paedophile and prostitution rings. Sethi said Belgium, Britain and Italy receive the youngest African girls, while Germany and Spain are major transit countries.

Child slavery, in which children are forced to work in very abject conditions, with little or no pay is spreading widely around the African continent, more than ever before. UNICEF estimates that 200,000 children from western and central Africa are sold into slavery each year, notably for seasonal work such as harvesting cocoa and other cash crops. In Ghana, under the Trokosi traditional practice, young girls are regularly given up as slaves to "atone" for crimes committed by other people in their families.

The issue of domestic child servitude—the modern day Cinderella syndrome, in which children are subjected to the worst forms of labour within the home, most of the time under very exploitative and abusive conditions, is very prevalent in most African countries. Many children who are trafficked within the West African sub-region usually under atrocious conditions, end up feeding the domestic labour market in the main urban centres of countries like Cote d'Ivoire, Gabon, Equitorial Guinea and the Congo. The case of Nigeria is once again particular. According to the Child Welfare League of Nigeria, with the presence of a child domestic servant in virtually every household, Nigeria could be seen to have the largest number of child domestic workers in the world. Majority of these children end up being physically, emotionally and if they are girls, sexually abused.

There are more tales of woe. Out of the 300,000 child soldiers around the world, it is estimated that 120,000 of these are African children who have been forced and recruited to take part in wars and fighting in some African countries. Sudan, Sierra Leone, Uganda, Rwanda and Burundi, to name a few African countries, are all shamed by the tragedy of child soldiers. The nature of child participation in wars ranges from active combat to support roles such as spying, mine-clearance and manning checkpoints. Young girls are made to provide sexual services for adult combatants. Since armed conflict does not discriminate in terms of gender or age, child soldiers often suffer greatly from the physical and psychological effects of violent conflict. They are exposed to atrocities such as mass murder, torture and sexual abuse. Under the influence of drugs and alcohol, often they are the perpetrators of such brutality, some time against their own family members.

Sexual exploitation, in which under-age young children are forced or cajoled into sex sometimes under the guise of marriage, is also on the increase. Most of these young children end up emotionally and physically damaged. Some of them develop terrible conditions like Vesico Vaginal Fistula (VVF). Others end up being infected with diseases such as HIV and other sexually transmitted diseases.

Experts have blamed the sudden rise in child abuse cases on the terrible economic conditions in Africa, which has led to a high level of poverty especially in the poor, rural parts of the continent. This means some parents, in order to relief the suffering, are often willing for their children to move away, sometimes to live with a better off relative. Ignorant of the possible dangers, they do this believing their child would be properly looked after. Usually, the opposite happens (Ariyo Debbie, internet article).

South Asia

While certain child abuse and neglect issues are common in almost all countries at the global level such as physical abuse, sexual abuse, emotional and psychological abuse, problems of street children, there are also many issues which are prevalent only in certain regions of the world. For instance, in Asia where population density is high, the issues of child labour and child sexual exploitation are also high. The largest population of children in the world live in South Asia and majority of these children lack access to proper health care, nutrition and education. This reflects the socio-economic reality of the developing countries of the Asian region. The main factors that contribute to the magnitude of the problem of child abuse are poverty, illiteracy, caste system, landlessness, lack of economic opportunities, rural-urban migration, population growth, political instability and weak implementation of legal provisions. If we go through the statistics regarding the rate of child harassment, it throws an egregious remark on the face of Asian countries. WHO estimates that almost 53,000 child deaths in 2002 were due to child homicide. In the Global School Based Student Health Survey carried out in a wide range of developing countries, between 20 per cent and 65 per cent of school going children reported having been verbally or physically bullied in school. Similar rates of bullying have been found in industrialized countries. An estimated 150 million girls and 73 million boys under 18 have experienced forced sexual intercourse or other forms of sexual violence involving physical contact. Some states in India among which a large portion of it currently under poverty line are Bihar, Uttar Pradesh, Odisha, Manipur and Mizoram and among these states the cases of child abuse and exploitation are occurring at increasing rates. The need for awareness for the same is more in these states where education is not given any primary importance and children are forced to work at early stages of life.

The International Labour Organisation estimates that worldwide there are 246 million children between 5 and 17 engaged in hazardous employment in drug trade, illegal arms trade, prostitution, pornography and as mercenary (Ram Sankar Singh 2009:6). According to the World Health Organisation, 20 per cent of women and 5-10 per cent of men report being sexually abused as children, while 25-50 per cent of all children report being physically abused.

Child Abuse and the Social Context

Child abuse, when it happens within or around the child's own immediate environment, the perpetrators are individuals known to the child—sometimes even trusted hands. Here the problem is individual and qualitative. However, the social context within which abuse takes place cannot be ignored. This follows that objective statements on child abuse are disputable.

Violence and abuse within the family have been looked at from medical, legal and psychological perspectives. Each perspective leads to the construction of a different definition. Child maltreatment hasn't been looked at as a socio-psychological and cultural problem. Specific societal circumstances can make a person abusive, who might not act in a similar manner in an environment that doesn't promote the thought.

The emphasis on individual freedom in the Western and American societies has been decisive in the relationship within and outside the family. The stringent rules regarding child abuse and protection are the outcome of individualism which is a social construct. But behavioural patterns in abusive families to some extent mirror societal attitudes. Moreover child abuse cannot be isolated from the larger social and cultural institutions that unwittingly encourage it (Gil, D.G. 1975). According to many social scientists, the causes of child abuse can gradually disappear if fundamental changes occur in the societal attitudes, values and human relations; it also might diminish with the elimination of socio-economic inequalities.

Who is the Abuser?

According to Spinetta (1972), in the Western Europe and the USA research on child abuse began in the context of a socio-cultural change effected by the second world war. What motivated the abuser was the topic of enquiry. It was found that a good many of the abusers were individuals within the family of the abused. The relationship between abuser's particular behaviour and the act of abuse could be ascertained with a personality study (Fieldman 1982). "Psychopathological studies" of Kempe (1972) Pollock (1968), Gelles and Kornell (1985) have found that Emotional deformities of individuals can lead to child abuse. Certain mental conditions, peculiar traits in the character, use of alcohol and sensual drugs have also to do with abusive behaviour (Wolfe 1987:45). The childhood experiences, neglect in the childhood, loneliness and deprivation, also cause the tendency to abuse. Prevailing socio-cultural circumstances can turn children mutually abusive (Wirani 2000). According to Spinetta (1972), the aggressive behaviour leading to abuse is the result of deformities in character. And deformities in character itself are the result of multiple causes, including genetic ones. (E.g. Some reports on the Arushy murder case indicate that the abusive parents killed their daughter for some reason and put the blame on others.) Parents might become abusive if their own emotional needs haven't been heeded or if they are not sufficiently emotionally mature, or they are unable to keep pace with the rate of growth of their ward, or due to the impurities that had crept into their own making through bad parenting (Wolfe 1987:45).

It is generally found that some parents and care givers have a tendency to find faults with their wards. They either do not like attending to the needs of their children or after verbally or physically harming them might come out with unsound justifications. Sometimes they may try to hide an injury inflicted upon their ward by another person; they may even not bother as to who caused the injury. They enforce a discipline that the child cannot bear. Such abusive people might have in their childhood suffered abuse, or might not have received filial love and protection, with the result that there is turbulence within them. They are the ones who are not able to hold control over their emotions, who lack self-respect. Some of them will be under severe financial pressures. There are also those who are psychopaths who have an innate tendency to harm every one. Sloan Irving (1983) has recorded several such traits of abusive parents and care givers.

The Traits of the Abuser

William Goode (1971:624-36) says that the following category of people can be abusive:

Those who are low in education

Those who consider themselves of low in status

Those who are low income and low status

Those who lack living learning skills.

Indicators of Abusive Individuals

The sexually abusive individuals are those who have not achieved conjugal contentment in their married life, who are emotionally ill-balanced, widowers, those with too many members in the family, addicts of alcohol and drugs, or those leading a solitary life distanced from social activities.

Although it is highly probable that psychopaths and those with abnormal behaviour could be child abusers, it hasn't been proven beyond doubt that it is their general nature (Wolfe 1985:462-82). Yet, the impulsive, the imbalanced, and the depressed are more likely to be abusive. Stress and depression have pulled the victims away from a right attitude to parenting. This happens not only due to the psychological ills that have come down genetically or the unhappy and turbulent childhood, but also due to the influence of unethical environment brought in by cultural changes initiated by a process broadly termed as globalization (Wise, J.M. 2008:57).

In a study like this it is only logical to enquire as to why the magnitude of child abuse is so high wherever it happens. The civilized world is so full of man-made problems that total awareness is difficult to achieve. All the man-made problems and other calamities affect the mind and body of the lay individual.

The imbalance in the distribution of wealth is not a modern phenomenon. But the social system under capitalism attracts everyone to profit and wealth and through that, power; the world is now witnessing a race to accumulate wealth which can buy comfort and pleasure. Ethics and morals are therefore sidelined. Moral degeneration, lack of respect for the fellow being, shall lead to the kind of chaos Ruth Cohn perceives: "A so-called 'nature of the human being' which propagates the right of the stronger is misleading, because its extended arm of destruction, not guided by ethical values, will destroy human kind together with our planet, if we do not discover a truly humane direction" (Cohn Ruth C. 2010).

Neglecting parents might be parents with troubled family life, living in insecure circumstances. They might be addicted to alcohol or drugs. They might be men and women with not sufficient emotional or intellectual growth to bring up children. They might be people who are not able to receive satisfaction from work, emotionally dissatisfied, and without self-confidence.

However in the society which is the target of this study not every act of punishment is abusive, nor is the doer abuser in the general perception of abuse.

Troublesome children are sometimes beaten and denied food even by parents who really love them. Such acts in the context of the culture of the communities under consideration cannot be termed as abuse. They are employed as measures to correct the 'errant child'. Moreover, in the previous two centuries, in this society the village school masters used to punish children under their tutorship severely for even minor errors, as is evident in the autobiography of the social reformer Mannathu Padmanabhan (quoted elsewhere). Such punishments although rigorous in nature were considered normal even by the parents. Even now in the Schools in the state, 'cane' is used as tool to discipline the students. Children in many schools have revealed that they are beaten as a punitive measure. A retired IAS officer who was the Director of Public Instructions in Kerala said that during his tenure as DPI he once gave a bundle of thirty canes (sticks) to the Head Master of a Government High School in the heart of Ernakulam (Kochi) city, and asked him to make full use of the sticks in thirty days. Since punishments of this kind were common in this state, this cannot be categorized 'abusive', although currently there is a move to ban flogging at school.

While pondering over the problem of child sexual abuse Pinky Wirani (2000) observes: "CSA happens because the system of silence around the act perpetuates it. CSA happens because this system of silence encourages some more men to want it to happen; and so the political, societal, cultural and religious attitudes which serve to underestimate the child, especially the female child, create a climate in which abuse can thrive." The long-term effects of child sexual abuse can lead to a number of personality disorders and mental health problems; the abused usually becomes an abuser (Wirani 65-67).

Some mothers do not take immediate protective actions even when they are aware of the abuse for reasons ranging from shame to financial security (Wirani 68). While law could be framed to declare abusive persons guilty and be brought before the court of law, *what lies at the root cannot be eliminated* without change in outlook and approach. The abusive state of mind could be the product of abused senses; the sensory ills could be the result of a society obsessed with the accumulation of personal wealth to the detriment of the general well-being (Charles Fourier 1851). Where human interaction is subordinated to a relationship between things, life is not humanly organized to allow a real form of common life, resulting in alienation. Mere consciousness of this is not enough. (Karl Marx, 1844, *Excerpt Notes*). In a money crazy consumerist society, relationship between individual and individual becomes relationship between individual and commodity. Thus, an adult looks at a child as commodity. A child who grows into an adult in such circumstances sees around him only commodities, not the human environment. The eyes are exposed to lights that flood into them; the ears frequently drummed into with sounds they are not expected to receive; the gases they cannot smell enter into the noses every second; the skin is laden with intolerable chemicals; what gets into the mouth is strange to the nature of taste buds and palate. The sense organs as a whole are thus estranged from their nature with the intervention of the artificially constructed. A human being who is a victim of consumerist culture is thus alienated from the nature of his own senses. His behaviour is bound to remain unnatural until balance is restored. There is every chance of his becoming abusive, because his own senses are abused.

Defects in parent-child interaction might lead to abuse. Factors operative in the society interact with those in the family to set an attitude to children. Interaction may be healthy in many cases, but not in every case. The ideal situation of parent offspring relationship is abstract, concrete reality in this case is problematic. The parent who carries the burns of past might not tolerate an over demanding child. Modern medical treatment has enabled many an infant from early death, who otherwise might not have survived. Such individuals might live with deformities, reproduce, and later find themselves incapable of facing the complexities of bringing up children. These parents tend to neglect, reject or abuse their children (Burgess 1979).

Cultural abuse—the television: Researchers have found that television cultivates exaggerated sense of danger and mistrust among regular viewers of crime-sex-suspense dramas. The children are vulnerable to beliefs based on what they are visually and auditorily exposed to at a regular basis. They develop violence related fears, mistrust people, and tend to fancy becoming one they see on the screen. The TV shows are market oriented, they feign educating the young, but don't really aim at educating them. The image that children get of themselves is that of a powerless minority, ill-treated by malevolent adults, who are perpetually in need of a saviour. Another image is that of an upstart child bully capable of braving any criminal and thereby himself becoming one. "The need is for action toward creating a culture, and television system that can afford to address itself to nation's future, its children" (Gerbner, George 1980:248).

Limitations of Data Collection—The Case of USA

While talking about Child Abuse Data in the United States, Jim Hopper (2009) comes out with the following important observations:

- Only recently, and only in particular countries and cultures, has the abuse of children come to be seen as a major social problem and a main cause of many people's suffering and personal problems.
- Of course children have been abused throughout human history. But for people to think about child abuse as we do now, to create legal definitions and government agencies that can remove children from their homes, and to conduct thousands of research studies on the effects of abuse—these are historically and culturally embedded developments.
- Some believe that, for the first time in history, we are beginning to face the true prevalence and significance of child abuse. Others worry that many people have become obsessed with child abuse and deny any personal responsibility for their problems while "blaming" them on abuse and bad parenting (I believe that each view has some validity).
- Clearly, then, some very large contexts and controversies shape debates about particular issues concerning child abuse.

He holds that

- Statistics on rates of child abuse and neglect are controversial.

- All statistics on the incidence and prevalence of child abuse and neglect are disputed by some experts. (Incidence refers to the number of new cases each year, and prevalence to the percentage of people in a population who have had such experiences.)

In his opinion the disputes on child abuse statistics arise due to the fact that

- Complex and subtle scientific issues are involved in studies that generate these statistics.
- Even the most objective scientific research is imperfect. At least one or two methods used in any study must be chosen by researchers based on opinions and judgements, not just facts and logic. The objectively best methods available may still have limitations.
- For example, there are important controversies about how to define abuse and neglect. This is true for official government studies and any other research study.
- The definitions of abuse used in official government studies are based on laws, because government definitions are needed for more than research purposes. They are also needed for purposes like determining whether or not suspected abuse should be reported, investigated, "substantiated" (as actually having occurred), and lead to action by a social service agency or court.
- In contrast, independent researchers can use different definitions because they have different purposes than government agencies, like understanding the different effects of mild and extreme emotional, physical, and/or sexual abuse.
- No matter what kind of study it is, small changes in definitions can result in big differences in statistics on abuse and neglect.

So far the perspective has been mainly the external scenario where the issues have been chiefly international. Child abuse is a serious subject in both developing and developed countries. In the developed countries, abuse results out of the shortcoming of the immediate, personal, environment. Whereas in some parts of Africa and Asia, apart from the personal anomalies in the immediate perpetrator, chaotic social atmosphere also draws children into hazardous, abusive, conditions.

Child Abuse in Kerala: An Overview

2

In India, traditional values used to underpin the relationship between the members of the joint family. In a typical traditional Indian family children are expected to be docile and obedient. Their role is to bring honour to their families by exhibiting good behaviour and high achievement and by contributing to the overall enhancement of the family. The female is forever dependent right from her birth. Children in general are dependent emotionally and often socially, on their parents, for the duration of the parents' lives. Traditionally, all difficulties are handled within the family. All members including children are expected to be selfless and obligated to significant others. Furthermore, one's behaviour should never bring shame to oneself or one's family (Segal Uma 1996:267).

Into this system which was supposed to be there forever going without change, the new ideology of the consumerist crept in seducing the adolescents into their culture. Thus, the consumerist children (and adolescents) consume drugs, porn and Western media that corrupt them. Here it becomes a problem which is a struggle within Indian society. The apparent seduction of youngsters by foreign cultural forces is, therefore, perceived as a threat to the entire culture and way of life. "Youth are seen as pushing their boundaries too far. And since adolescence is a period when children finish their socialization process, this also means that they are not fully socialized. Meaning that they are too unstable, impetuous, emotional, and dangerous, having not yet fully embedded the social within their habits of thought and body" (Wise, J.M. 2008:58).

Kerala—Child Abuse and the Geographic, Historic, Cultural and Demographic Context

The foregoing was a glimpse at the Indian scenario. The focus being on the predicament of children in the State of Kerala, a brief introduction to the land and its people will help place the problem in the proper context.

Geographical location has enabled Kerala to maintain a socio-cultural tradition unique to itself. Between the Sahya mountains and the Arabian sea, to the southwest of peninsular India, Kerala is a narrow stretch of land of 38,863 square kilometres. For convenience the land is identified into three regions: the highland or the hilly region with dense vegetation and animals, the midland and the coastal region dominated by human habitation (the land slopes down from the mountains, that is from the east to the west, dividing Keralam into what is locally called *malanadu*, *idanadu* and *theerabhoomi*).

In the past the region was comparatively free of military raids barring ones by the Kings of Thamizhakam. Therefore, the land's culture and heritage remained intact until the arrival of the Portuguese in the late fifteenth century. Thereafter Hyder and Tippu in the north and the British in the whole of region brought turbulence that had decisive impact on the social setup (Menon 2007).

Geographically, present day Kerala State (Keralam) is only 1.2 per cent of the Indian union. The appearance of the villages of Keralam is different from those in other parts of India. While in the villages elsewhere in India the houses are huddled together, houses in the villages here are scattered or isolated dwellings. Perhaps because of its geographical isolation this region was only infrequently threatened by invaders and bandits which enabled the people live an open communal life. With their seemingly isolated households the Kerala villages had a well knit social structure with village schools, smithy and carpentry, medical system and agricultural production. The modern villages have high schools and even colleges, hospitals, public library, organised labour and centres of religious worship. In fact, Kerala is an elaborate township for the most part, but with a rural flavour. It is said that the only city of Kerala with the distinguishing marks of urban life is Kochi. The rest of them, Kozhikode and the capital city Thiruvananthapuram, still retain traits of village life.

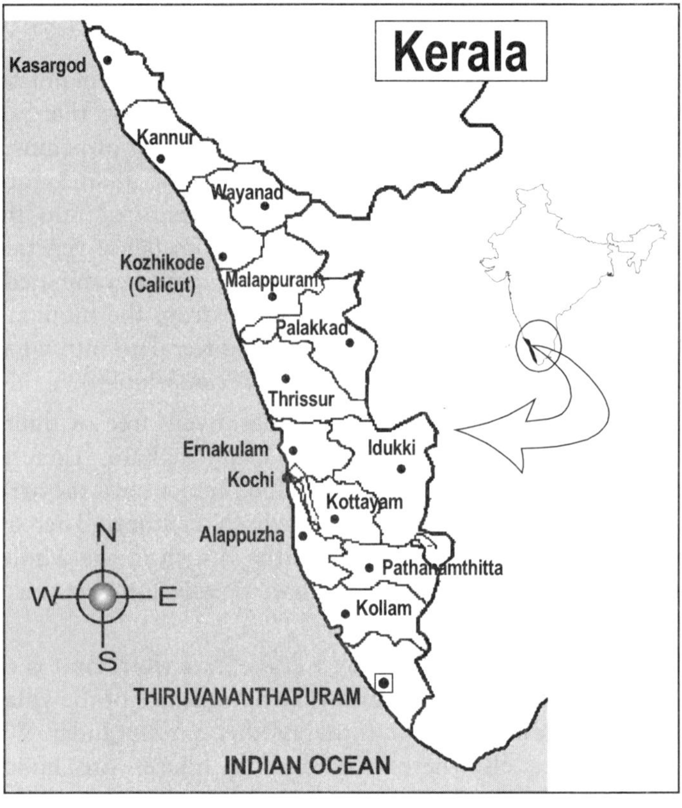

Kerala-geographical size (percentage)

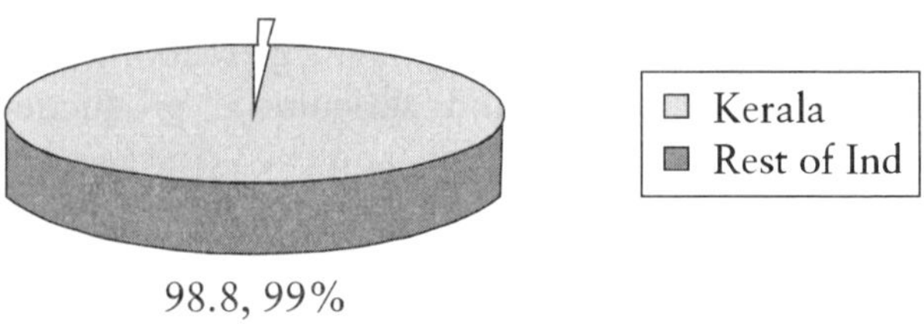

A major difference between the different communities in Kerala and Northern India is that traditionally the majority of the communities in Kerala haven't been patriarchal. Communities like the Nairs were matrilineal till the early decades of the 20th century. The switch over to the patriarchal system has been difficult, the after-effects of which are still perceptible. The known history of the region has proof to the fact that people of this region, although like the rest considered children their property, cared for their well-being by giving them basic education. This attitude, to this investigator's knowledge, paved the way to what is currently known as the Kerala model of development.

Elamkulam Kunjan Pillai, an authority on the ancient history of Kerala, maintains that education was universal in Kerala till the fifth century AD. Children and women belonging to all the different communities (tribes) received education. However, with the advent of the four caste system things turned for the worse. Casteism led to discrimination and exploitation of the meek and the weak (Elamkulam 267). Sreedhara Menon also means almost the same when he observes that children without gender difference received education during the Sangha period, but not for long (Menon 77-78). Although generations had trodden through the dark corridors of history, the people could still catch up with the rest of the world in matters concerning education. There was steady social progress after the awakening initiated by reformers like Chattambi Swamikal, Sreenarayana Guru, and Ayyan Kali in the late nineteenth century.

Available records on the abuse of children in Kerala and denial of education to lower castes could be traced to the 1860s (Samuel Mateer, 1870).

> Vernacular schools conducted by private teachers [*asan pallikkoodam*] were found in almost every village in Travancore...in most of these schools there are from 20 to 30 or more boys. I was pleased to find in almost every school from 2 to 4 or 5 Sudra girls and Ilavar girls.... Schools supported by the native government are of superior class.... In the junior Depatment of [the High

> School] nearly 700 boys of all castes except the lowest receive a good English education.... Female education too is spreading. There has never been any decided objection on the part of sudras or elavas to the elementary instruction of females. One to two thousand girls of these castes attend the ordinary village schools.... Of course the lowest classes are without the means of obtaining instruction except in Mission Schools; their children being denied admission to all respectable native schools, and with rare and recent exceptions, in government schools. (Mateer 1870:155-57)

Children belonging to a good portion of the population could thus take advantage of elementary education in the Kerala of the second half of the nineteenth century. Yet the same society of the period could not but allow its unfortunate children to be sold for paltry amounts:

> The number of persons originally reduced to a state of slavery was increased by the sale of children in the times of famine and distress, which has occurred even in our own day [the 1860s] (297). During the famine of 1860, Mr. Cox wrote "the people are selling their own children, and this for a mere trifle...for a quarter of a rupee or less, they sell their children to the Mohammedans and others on the sea coast; and these have means of disposing them again so as to make much profit—of course they make converts of them at once...." A century ago [in the 1760s] a similar practice was described by Forbes "The number of poor people coming down to Anjengo and other sea ports from the inland country during a famine, either to sell themselves or to dispose of their children as slaves is astonishing." (Mateer 1883:299-300)

This implies that the history of at least two hundred years doesn't give bright picture of childhood in Kerala; inequality of the socio-economic kind was at its height which put the weak into a perilous plight; the low caste people were treated like cattle, their children were the property of their mother's master and were put to work—"Not having proper food, the children are weak and unable to do hard work; therefore they are not paid any wages until they are fifteen years of age" (Mateer 1883:303). Perhaps the State is ironically named as "god's own country".

In the nineteenth century and in the early twentieth century children at elementary schools run by village schoolmasters were physically maltreated by the teachers called *asans*. Mannathu Padmanabhan, the founder of the Nair Service Society, and T.K. Madhavan, a leader of the Sreenarayana Dharma Paripalana movement, testifie with their own experiences that those village school masters believed that torture had many good effects (*thadanat bahavo guna*). Mannam observes,

> As it was well known that the punishment for truancy and defiance was to have one's fingers crossed and hands bound together by a coir rope and hung from the roof of the school shed, even the most troublesome and disobedient student readily obeyed his teacher. It was said that under the student hung from the roof, a fire would be lit, and at its centre, the stylus would be placed with its sharp tip pointing upwards. In these circumstances every care would be taken by one subjected to this punishment to ensure that his hands do not give way. I have heard that some guardians used to help the teachers to carry out this punishment. (Mannam 1998:4-5)

Sri Madhavan writes in his memoir that the village school he attended during his childhood had a heartless master who caned him fiercely even as the child Madhavan bled profusely from a new wound on the left cheek (Madhavan 1954:31).

With the demise of the matrilineal system in Kerala, nuclear families sprouted in large numbers, through a chain of bifurcations resulting in families with ill trained heads (Gough E. Kathleen 1993). To maintain hold on the members many family heads resorted to maltreatment of wife and children.

Till not long ago, maltreatment of children was not looked at as a social problem worthy of attention. For the same reason the psychological impact that anger of very high degree had on children, whether by parents or caretakers or teachers, was not taken seriously by the society. Even at this level of awareness regarding rights, within and outside the family, without rural urban distinction, children are subject to abuse. This is due to the prevalence of high degree of stress caused by different aspects of modern life.

"Even if you have only one child beat him with the wooden pestle." However, there is another saying which means that the child wouldn't die even if the mother steps on him. This is indicative of the intensity of the maternal care; socially sanctioned and ethically relevant punishments were not supposed to retard the growth of the child. Yet lack of resources to provide the bare necessities, lack of education and lack of birth control were definite causes of child neglect and other attitudes of carelessness towards the child in the past. The parent who as child received physical and mental torture tends to abuse. The prevailing social conditions that encourage alcoholism and drugs, occupational stress, and the attitudinal change in the family caused by the several factors (socio-economic, cultural, ethical) have created an environment conducive to abuse (Belsky 1980).

That the traditional attitude to child rearing in Kerala was stringent, is sounded high in the local belief that parents have the right to treat their child the same manner they were treated as children (Bandura 1973). Gil (1970) thinks that the act of child abuse is linked to the social class and the size of the family. Historians of Kerala like Elamkulam Kunjan Pillai (1970) maintain that the children were stress free in the joint families. The adult respondents who provided data are almost unanimous in their identification of the 'nuclear family' as a major factor causing child abuse. The nature of abuse depends to a considerable extent upon the internal as well as external environment of the family of the abused, or the environment in which the abused happens to be. If the environment is not congenial the children can be victims. Those children who are not good at studies, who are self-centred and obstinate will be the more victimized (Garbarino 1977).

Now there is noticeable change in the ethics of Kerala society. This could be attributed to the imbalance created by the 'changes' accompanying globalization. The global interpenetration of chains of causation is connected with each individual who lives in a nation under its impact. When each economically rich country of the West and America strikes on the developing countries at a singular moment, the impact is as many times as the number of countries striking. This has no comparison with what it was in the past. The hegemony is still capitalistic, its interests are on profit at the expense of human and earth communities (Peters, R.T. 2008:64). Globalization of the kind that we experience in our country places emphasis on individualism and profit, which fuel corruption, disparity and abuse. People's choices to live productive and creative lives according to their needs and interests—to focus on the lives that people have reason to value (Amartya Sen 1999) have lost place in the ethics of the day in this part of the peninsula.

While looking for what lies at the root of the trend to look at every thing as commodity, along with the ethical issues we will find the disparity in the distribution of poverty in the context of economic liberalization and the lure of media to the 'comforts' and 'pleasures' that money can bring through constant virtual presentation of the 'culture' of the economically rich societies as factors adding to the socio-cultural imbalance noticeable in this region. The caprice of the economically advanced societies might appear appallingly disturbing to the economically underdeveloped. In our world today, basic education for everyone would cost $6 billion while currently Americans spend $8 billion annually on cosmetics; water and sanitation for everyone in the world would cost $9 billion while Europeans annually spend $11 billion on ice cream; providing reproductive health care for all women in the world would cost $12 billion, Americans and Europeans combined currently spend that much annually on perfumes; basic health and nutrition for everyone in the world would only cost $13 billion and yet, Europeans and Americans spend $17 billion annually on pet food (UNDP 1998:37). These rates of consumption betray moral indifference to the plight of the poor. The Capitalists see only market, not life. The third world is a market where they can sell everything.

Neoliberal Capital and Violation of Child Rights in Kerala

According to an assessment (Jozsef Borocz 2005) in Gross National Per Capita Income (2000), India stood among the poor countries with 2810 US$ which was roughly one-seventh of the GNI/cap of the US (19635 US$) and even lower than that of Sri Lanka (3010 US$). Kerala, over the years, has advanced economically with a per capita income well above the national average, with its educated labour force bringing money from jobs abroad.

Progress of the State of Kerala that had low per capita income has been the contribution of a liberal policy on education followed even by the erstwhile monarchs of the state of Travancore. Of late the State has become victim of commoditization of education, earmarked by the mushrooming of self-financing educational institutions that focus mainly on profit-making.

Pedophilia in Kerala

Pedophilia is a punishable immoral act. This fact is perhaps not known to a sizeable section of the Kerala society. While attempting to collect data from the northern part of Kerala in December 2009, this investigator met J.J. Pallath, a former Christian priest currently working as the Director of Jeevan Samskrithi, an NGO attached to the Kerala State Aids Control Society. This NGO deals with the male prostitutes and MSMs of Kannur district. An unpublished project report of this NGO contains extraordinary findings on sexual abuse among male children below eighteen and of the pedophilic kind of abuse rampant in the dominant 'business community' of the region that has made cultural subscriptions from abroad.

> The investigator [Pallath] discovered that there is a sort of deification of semen among the [b.community]. They use the semen of young boys, below twenty is believed to be the best, as a cosmetic cream for applying on the face. They spill the semen of young boys on the face and sleep; swallowing the semen of young boys is considered to be the best tonic for perfect health. Thus the young boys get initiated into oral sex very early in life.... This investigator

> discovered through participant observation in some of the most thickly populated [b.community] areas that the most venerated images by the boys [of that community] is the penis.... From the interviews the investigator discovered that not many boys who are handsome are left without same sex experience by the time they are twelve.... There is no time and place for it , even in the [place of worship] when electricity fails, seniors engage in sex with the boys. (Pallath 2004:97)

According to the above investigator, a good number of the religious teachers belonging to this community of northern Kerala are habitual pedophiles. He cites the evidence of an erstwhile Member of Parliament from Kannur belonging to the community referred to who has openly admitted that in his early boyhood he was sexually abused by his religious teacher. The ex-M.P. also observed that these religious teachers do this invariably with children who attend their classes (Pallath 2004:98). This may appear odd and highly immoral to many; but this is there, and known to many in the community in which this happens.

Victims of trafficking are usually with unstable homes or economically weak background with high rate of illiteracy and little social mobility. Women and children are the most affected when compared to men because in such areas they are the weakest and therefore vulnerable. The official figure of trafficking is not available, but police crime records on disappearance/abduction show that Malappuram district of Kerala tops in disappearance due to abduction. This does not include children of both sex trafficked under various pretexts.

Kerala: The Present Context

In Kerala, as everywhere in India, the belief is that the parents are devout to the well-being of their children. Reality of the day contradicts this traditional belief around parenthood. The event that led to the conception of the idea behind this project took place in October 2007 at Santhanpara in Idukki District. Benny, a young man and Manju his wife used to leave Aromal their male child in chains with a dog, as they went on daily work away from home. When police unchained the three-year-old, he was in a sorry state with palms swollen out of burning. The child had marks of burnt injuries with cigarette stumps and signs of whacking with a cane. Benny had claimed that he had the right to do anything with his child. Now the parents are under trial for attempting to kill the child.

There are parents who abuse their female children from a very early stage and before maturity throw into situations more deplorable than are found in so-called red streets. Complaints used to come up earlier regarding girls trapped by their distant female relatives in the name of providing them with the kind of job they might be aspiring to get and then leaving them with some brothel. From Paravoor in Ernakulam district, Police registered cases against a girl's father and mother on grounds of sexual abuse and flesh trade. The father was the first abuser who later forced the child into flesh trade. He later took his daughter, a first year higher secondary student, to a number of clients hoodwinking her with chances of an opening in cinema or TV serial. From that time on he has handed her over to several clients. K.G. Babu, Circle Inspector of Police, Paravoor took him into custody under charges of sexual assault of minor. The girl's mother was arrested for suppression of fact. It is quite surprising to note that the people who have declared devotion to public welfare—Eldo K. Mathew [CPI(M) local leader of of Puthenkuris, in Ernakulam] and Thomas Varghese [CPI(M) local secretary of Mazhavannoor, Ernakulam]—were nabbed by the Police for sexually abusing the girl. (cf. *Mathrubhoomi*, Editorial, 6 July 2011.)

Incidents of mothers pushing their daughters into the flesh market are not rare. In Ambalapuzha in Alappuzha district a mother took her under eighteen daughter to a lodge for flesh trade (Report in *Mathrubhoomi*, March 2011). Father and mother, whose accountability is absolute in the physical and mental well-being of the children, have traditionally been placed along with *guru* and *god*. For the consumerist society everything including the child is a commodity. Moral duty is subordinate to the cravings of the body, it is less significant and therefore the adults who are parents seem to have stepped down from the high pedestal. Politicians who were erstwhile champions of the poor have turned out to be opportunists who would not miss a chance to abuse an unfortunate girl. This gives out that poverty is not the only reason for abuse. This necessitates moral and aesthetic education made compulsory part of school and college education.

This has happened even after the bills protecting children from exploitation have been passed by the parliament. Therefore the problem is not lack of rules or laws. When law takes its own course, the culprits use money and power to influence witnesses and even the complainant. There will be sufficient 'loop holes' in the FIR, and in the very manner in which the case is presented before the court. When the case is postponed a number of times, the culprits make use of the loopholes to escape. The law is strong, but the manner of execution takes its vitality away. An end to the indefinite delays in the court proceedings would be a welcome event.

'What is it that instigates the parents to throw their own children into hopelessness?' was a question raised in the editorial of a daily newspaper in Malayalam? Is it extreme poverty? If it is lack of employment the cause, how come young men from the northeast of India arrive here in large numbers for work. It is not always lack of food or cloth or medicine that motivates the men and women take the wrong track. Many of them are alcoholics or drug addicts. Even in broad daylight in less frequented country roads and lanes female children are unsafe. Young girls are greatly excited at an offer to work in a cinema or TV serial and not knowing what lies ahead they walk into the vicious circle. The abusers belong to all sections of the society, they belong to all walks of life. This makes the issue all the more complex. It appears that neither education nor high ranking position makes an individual morally or ethically strong. Exposing and educating the masses about this wild treachery is the job ahead of social workers ("What happened to our society?" Editorial. *Mathrubhoomi*, July 6, 2011).

Adolescent sex crimes are reported daily in the newspapers: "In Kolencherry a 13-year-old boy who sexually abused his maternal cousin of his own age was nabbed by the Police, along with two other accused who are the victim's classmates." "In Palodu a third standard student belonging to an Adivasi community was sexually abused by three male students" (*Mathrubhoomi* 7 July 2011). Certainly the deteriorating state of moral and ethical values is reflected in the innumerable examples of the above kind. The immediate identifiable causes are the increasing craze for pleasure, lack of restraint induced by exposure to excesses on internet and mobile phone; alcoholism and drug addiction; watching TV dramas and near porn advertisements.

Horrendous hiring of wombs for the production of babies for sale has become the latest trend in child abuse in Kerala. The state police has found that this happens under the cover of home for destitute children, and home nursing establishments. An advocate from Aluva in Ernakulam district and his woman accomplice were arrested in this connection. Police say that the racketeers pay rupees fifty thousand to the womb-lender. They said this team had already sold twenty children born in this manner. The Police aren't yet sure who the buyers are and to what purpose they are used. At present children are used in child beggary, child labour, child prostitution, and most horribly for sale of organ. Children below five trafficked overseas are used as 'Jockeys' in camel race. They are tied on the camel's back. When they scream out of horror, the camels run faster. The children who tumble down are sometimes trampled to death. There is no strict monitoring of what happens in orphanages and homes for destitute children. There is no proper record of such centres. According to the official record there are 1674 orphanages in Kerala, out of which only a few have a healthy story to narrate. But there are no records available on the exact number of the unauthorized orphanages in the state. Many receive large unauthorized funds from foreign countries; left untracked, the money is used in abuse of greater dimensions like moulding the children into terrorists. (*Mathrubhoomi* 20 March 2011).

In Dec. 2010, the city Police Commissioner of Calicut Mr. P. Vijayan reported that the city Police have interrogated both boys and girls who have come under the influence of the drug sellers. The police found that a thirteen-year-old girl had scratched the words 'I hate myself' on her forearm, which her mother hadn't noticed. A survey conducted by IMHANS, a Kerala based NGO, concludes that 45 per cent of the child respondents were bored of life. They, like many other researchers, have found that children from homes where the parents quarrel appear distressed, and exhibit tendency to go off track. The police have observed from cases they handled that the age between 12 and 16 is the most vulnerable for boys and girls.

Many boys in the city of Calicut have become experts in stealing motorbikes with the expertise that might put to shame even the professionals in the field. Their parents never asked how they got the bike. And those who asked were satisfied with the lie the boys told them even when they knew the truth be contrary. And some parents ignore, or blatantly support their children in whatever they do. A sixteen-year-old boy from Calicut who the police intercepted was the member of a 'quotation gang' (a criminal gang that undertakes criminal jobs such as beating, mutilation or killing for certain amount). His parents had broken off relationship. His mother was a strict person. To act as foil to her the father used to give him pocket full of money which finally led to his enlistment in the criminal gang at the tender age of sixteen. A fourteen-year-old girl, an eighth class student, belonging to the same locality used to leave home in the morning for her tuition classes. She used to attend these sessions, but didn't attend the school for several weeks, yet reached home on time. It was only when the school asked for an explanation that the parents bothered to inquire what was happening. The girl was in the grip of the drug mafia. The schools are frequented by retail drug sellers. The police have hooked hundreds of them. Hardly any school has complained about the presence of antisocial elements in their premises (*Courtesy*: article by P. Vijayan, City Police Commissioner, Calicut, in *Mathrubhoomi*, December 2010).

Head Mistress of Kazhakkoottam Govt. High School, in Trivandrum district informed this investigator that they are afraid of the Mafia and the politicians who protected them. The boys who belong to the family of the members of the local mafia and others who are bent on mischief are a threat to the rest of the children at school and the staff. This leads to fall in student strength—many parents withdraw their children from Government schools and put them in self-financing institutions. Contrary to this could be found in the northern district of Kannur—AKG Memorial Government HSS, Peralassery, has an excellent record of discipline, good results and good student strength. This is possible here because the school has the blessings of a local political outfit.

In March 2011, forty-nine-year-old Narasimha Nayak of Kundangara Kadukka, near Kumbala in Kasargod district was arrested by the Deputy Superintendent of Police, Mr. P. Vikraman, for sexually abusing 10 girls of a primary school in Kumbala. Mr. Nayak who is a professional gambler lured the children with offers of sweets and money. The girls were between 10 and 12 years of age. Childline officials to whom the teachers complained first said that the way the police interrogated the children wasn't fitting to the age of the children.

He who according to Indian ethics should be friend, philosopher and guide can easily become an abuser in Kerala, in the present social circumstances. The people in Kerala used to look at a teacher with veneration. But things seem to turn for the worse when teachers turn abusers. In early April 2011 Athanipadi Pandaravalappil Saithalavi, the Head Master of Kottathara G.M.U.P. School, in Thirur, Malappuram District was caught by police for sexually and emotionally abusing thirty students of the school. The DIG of police, Mr. Sreegith said that Saithalavi has been abusing both boys and girls for six months. (Report in *Mathrubhoomi*, 2-4-11).

In early May 2010, Aluva Police (Ernakulam district) filed a case against Advocate Imthias, son of former High Court Judge Shafi, and his wife Kamarunnisa, for torturing eleven-year-old Radha. The Girl from Theni in Tamil Nadu was bought from a broker when she was eight. She was under forced labour in miserable conditions for three years. On her chest she had marks of severe burn injuries with red hot iron. She used an opportunity to escape during a function at the former Judge's house, and made her way to Edathala Ambedkar colony where at Mr. Dasan's home she pleaded for help. Later she narrated the tale of torture to the Additional Superintendent of Police, K. Jayanath.

In February 2011 in Ernakulam, an eleven-year-old domestic help girl, Dhanalakshmi, died due to injuries inflicted on her by her employers Sindhu Nair and Jose Kurien. The girl bore signs of physical torture and sexual abuse. The doctors confirmed that the girl had starved, had wounds of torture including burns. Ernakulam police arrested the two accused, and two suspected middle persons—Nagappan, from Pondichery, who feigned as the uncle of the girl. The other, a Kerala woman Shyla Naser, allegedly supplied girls from poor Tamil families to work as domestic servants in Kerala. Sindhu and Kurien have been charged against crimes of forced child labour, sexual abuse and murder.

In the incidents cited abuse involved burning injuries. Etiologically, in India, unlike the cases of child abuse by burning in the west, there are more reported incidents of contact burn with hot appliances or with acids in older children.

> ...there are older children employed as domestic help. They are abused by burning with hot metal rods, and hot ladles are sometimes used to inflict strokes. When female children employed in households resist the sexual advances by their employers, they get punished by the slashing acid on the perineum. These girls suffer deep burns. Sometimes burning cigarette butts are used to inflict burn injuries on teenage girls for the same reason. (Mathangi Ramakrishnan, 2010)

The abusers of the kind cited were educated, financially sound who lead a comfortable material life in towns. Concealed under the external glitter there is wanton cruelty and lust. Educated people, parents and teachers are traditionally supposed to provide good models of righteous living for children. The two children, Radha and Dhanalakshmi, who were victims of abuse, belong to the category of children who either leave their homes due to extreme poverty and/or destitution. There are children whose parents sell them out of sheer poverty. The number of working children is on the increase. Yet in the official records on child labour put out not even half truths. In a state which boasts of high rate of literacy and education, child labourers are ill treated to an intolerable extent. This happens when there are not enough realistic laws to protect them.

The majority of the child beggars and helpers in the state who suffer untold miseries come from the neighbouring states. Many of the child beggars have been disfigured after they were kidnapped. The Kerala high court has instructed the state police to stop child beggary and to bring the perpetrators before the law. The child labour prohibition act, and the compulsory education act are intended to ensure security and education of children. The facts the events uncover signal that administration of the law is easier said than done. Those parents whose will power has been eaten up by sheer poverty sell their children expecting to save them by doing so. The way out is to eradicate poverty. The role of the state in this situation is to locate these children and deliver them back to the parents or to create a system that can take care of their rehabilitation in the manner described in the constitution.

Distress in School Going Children

Literacy being widespread in modern Kerala, the majority children belonging to all strata of society attend schools. As many of the married women too go to some work, there is no one at home when the child returns home. In the joint family there were grandparents, aunties and uncles—a child returning from school upset about something was soothed and comforted by the elders. But with the advent of the nuclear family the overwrought children returned from school to empty homes. The parents when they returned home were either tired or preoccupied with career hassles. The problem in the cities like Mumbai is very severe, with 26 juvenile suicides in one week (Kankana Basu, *The Hindu*, Feb. 7, 2010). The following observation is valid not only to a metropolis like Mumbai, but also to the towns and cities of Kerala:

- Parents in the cities blame the educational system that places examination above holistic learning, for juvenile depression. However, working parents believe that engaging children in a series of classes is safe for them.
- Psychologists maintain that in families where the parents go to work, there is poor emotional contact between parents and children; most of the children have bad dietary habits and poor sleep. They feel that filling the child's life with a series of classes could have adverse effects on their mental health. The days' sensory load has to be 'decluttered' so that the brain is free from load.
- It is a positive sign that at least some parents have begun to realize that happy children are more important than successful children; joint families were happy homes for children. And the specialists advise them to go back to old family values for good measure and move forward in a happy manner, fast forward to the past. (Kankana Basu, 2010)

While the foregoing is one facet of what modern living does to children in the cities, there is another that shares certain of these aspects while hinting at change in the frame of mind among parents marking excessive care. The context of modern living is also arbitrated by the technology that creates modern gadgets like the computer and the mobile phone. Attempting a brief assessment of the context, Siby Mathews IPS, ADGP of Kerala Police, observes that while nuclear families have become common, the village atmosphere is fast waning. The number of [houses has increased] children has come down. A good many of the parents are eager to give whatever comfort they can to the child—they bring them up like princes/princesses. They wish to send the child to the best school; get them motor bikes when he/she is just fourteen. The parents do not stop to think whether it is worthwhile for the child to grow not knowing the agonies of life. Children of these parents do not practise sharing and caring, nor do they know the grief of dearth and deprivation. These children live in a world prevailed by television, internet and mobile phones and unlike their predecessors who lived in the villages, know pretty well what is happening around. They keenly observe their parents and other elders. There is lack of role models, the archetypes to learn from. This worries them and upsets them. This is perhaps why they run after the modern pleasures [of drug, music, liquor and sex] (Siby Mathews IPS, ADGP of Kerala Police, Sept. 2010).

For some reason the human mind is now mutually intolerant, selfish and more cruel. Why is this so? Why does this happen?

Popularity of internet porn, indiscriminate display of nudity on television, loss of faith in virtues, the thought that there is nothing called morality are factors influencing life in Kerala. Alcohol and drugs affecting vital systems, chemically treated food, polluted air and water affecting the nervous system, loss of sleep, loss of ethical consideration, and the thought that money can buy prestige, comfort and pleasure have generated a socially toxic environment in the state.

Although the availability of per capita food in Kerala was much lower than in the rest of India in the sixties, the contribution of free schooling, nutritional programmes for children, and extension of public health facilities could make to the promotion of social mobility, demographic transformation, and the organizational power and bargaining strength of the underprivileged sections of the population. The supporting programmes in education like midday meals have helped to reduce the number of school drop-outs. A fairly high proportion of the children from the lower strata are now able to reach the final stage of school education, promoting considerable vertical social mobility. The significant downward trend in birth rate, reduction in infant and child mortality, rise in female education as evidenced in the census reports are the positive outcome of societal change. The fact that in the sixties Kerala was a relatively poor state in India when judged by conventional norms such as per capita income; that the average per capita availability of food was lower in Kerala than in most parts of

India; but that nevertheless it has been possible for the state to make fairly impressive advances in the spheres of health and education, and hence bring about improvements that have made a perceptible difference to the quality of life (UN/CDS, 1980: 147-53). The International Labour Organization in its report to G20 (2009) has lauded the Kerala model of the 1960s of spending 35 per cent of the total revenue on education, and through that achieving economic growth. (UN [Department of Economic and Social Affairs. Poverty, Unemployemnt and Development Policy. Reprint (1980) Thiruvananthapuram: CDS]). However, with the neo-liberal policies in vogue the achievements appear to have been marred by the loss in ethics and morals. Spurred by the craze for economic prosperity that began in the nineteen nineties the people of Kerala are now heading towards unhealthy social situations. This has stained the advantages wrought by education.

In the case of Kerala, idea of childhood or the period called so in the life of an individual, is not the same as it used to be some four or five decades ago. A fifty-year-old person's conception of childhood is based on what he experienced in his childhood. So the childhood of the first or second decade of the 21st century cannot be measured with the same yard-stick. Forty years ago children in the villages of Kerala found pleasure in country games such as the 'head-ball' and the adolescents took pleasure in reading detective fiction. Now there are the TV channels, internet, alcohol and drugs that fill the dreams of the growing generation. Their elders are happy in not observing secrecy in domestic matters. There are adults who celebrate the times with liquor, porn, internet, and cell phones. There is no wonder their children are a step ahead. So the treatment should begin with the source of the problem, the adults.

For reasons that might surface upon introspection by the adults, the family fabric has become threadbare. The children of the day receive their lessons in living from the tangled mess of relationships within and outside the family. Their socialization too doesn't happen as in the past. *Visha* and *amrit* are the byproducts of the same *yaga*. It is the value dominant in us that should decide the choice between the two. The individuals in the state in large numbers have opted for the capitalist consumerist way of life where money brings respectability; here the concepts of righteous living are conveniently forgotten. Individualism appears to have gained upper hand pushing down collective interest: self-centredness takes over, which means turning one's back on the values which were hitherto considered eternal. This is a fertile ground for abuse, where the weak are the easy victims. The choice depends on will, individual and collective, whether to have *amrita*, live and let live or be selfish and get lost in the labyrinth of *visha*. (Summary of the personal communication by Prof. T.K. Levan, Kannur 2011.)

The national study on child abuse (MWCD 2007), which complements the UN Secretary General's Global Study on Violence Against Children 2006, has provided statistics on the extent and magnitude of the various forms of child abuse in India. As the first comprehensive study of its kind in India, this has potential to provide incentive to research in the area.

Major Findings of the Study (MWCD 2007)

1. Across different forms of abuse, and across different abuse groups, the younger children, of the age group 5-12 have reported higher levels of abuse.
2. Persons in trust and authority are the major abusers. 70 per cent of abused child respondents never reported the matter to any one.

Physical Abuse

- Two out of every three children were physically abused.
- Out of 69 per cent of children physically abused in 13 sample states, 54.68 were boys.
- Over 50 per cent children in 13 sample states were being subject to one or other form of physical abuse.
- Out of those children physically abused in family situations, 88.6 per cent were abused by parents.
- 65 per cent of school going children reported corporal punishment, that is, two out of three children were victims of corporal punishment.

- 62 per cent of the corporal punishment was in Municipal/Government schools.
- The States of Andhra Pradesh, Assam, Bihar and Delhi have almost consistently reported higher rates in all forms of abuse than the other states.
- Most children did not report the matter to anyone.
- 50.2 per cent children worked seven days a week.

Sexual Abuse

- 53.22 per cent children reported one or more forms of sexual abuse.
- Andhra Pradesh, Assam, Bihar and Delhi reported the highest percentage of abuse among both boys and girls.
- 21.90 per cent of children reported severe forms of sexual abuse and 50.76 per cent other forms of sexual abuse.
- Out of the child respondents 5.69 per cent reported being sexually assaulted.
- Children in Andhra Pradesh, Assam, Bihar and Delhi reported highest incidence of sexual assault.
- Children on street, children at work and children in institutional care reported the highest incidence of sexual assault.
- 50 per cent abuses are by persons known to the child or in a position of trust and responsibility.
- Most children did not report the matter to anybody.

Emotional Abuse and Girl Child Neglect

- Every second child reported facing emotional abuse.
- Equal percentage of both boys and girls reported facing emotional abuse.
- In 83 per cent of the cases parents were the abusers.
- 48.4 per cent girls wished they were boys.

Present State of Abuse

The children in India are conditioned by the traditional social fabric into unquestioning obedience to their parents and elders. This in the context of attitudinal change and lack of proper ethics on the part of the adults have resulted in abuse of children. And even the elderly people endure abuse (Sugatha Kumari, 2010, Interview). The Nithari incident near India's national capital, where 38 children were allegedly raped and murdered in 2007, apart from cruelty, is a vector to the rate of apathy, indifference and, criminal neglect on the part of all concerned. When this happened near the administrative headquarters of the Indian State, the venom is spat in every direction. CSA is spreading like AIDS.

Tulir, Centre for the Prevention and Healing of Child Sex Abuse, Chennai, has come out with the following observation on the nature of child sex abuse:

- Children can never initiate sexual abuse. Terming a child's behaviour "seductive" is an adult justification, projection and misinterpretation.
- The majority of abusers are known to the child and are often in positions of trust and power *vis-à-vis* the child. Example: Family, relatives, neighbours, teachers, etc.
- Abusers are seldom mentally ill; on the contrary they are "regular" people who lead "routine" lives.
- Statistical data from available research and reported incidents (from children and adult survivors) clearly indicates that child sexual abuse is a widespread problem affecting an extremely large number of children in the country.
- Child sexual abuse occurs in all social and economic classes of society.
- Both girls and boys are victims.
- All children are vulnerable to sexual abuse. Research has proven that differently able children are in fact more likely to be abused because of their increased vulnerabilities.
- Children do not lie or weave stories about being sexually abused. The pressure to remain silent to uphold distorted concepts of honour and respect is

immense. Also, children in our society are kept ignorant of sex and the possibility of abuse. Given these two facts the child is not lying when he/she relates an incident of sexual abuse.

- Usually nobody is aware that the child is being sexually abused.
- Though most of abusers are men, a small number of women abuse children sexually.
- In most reported cases the abuser is not physically violent but uses emotional manipulation to coerce the victim.
- Child sexual abuse usually has harmful effects and can lead to behavioural, emotional, physical and interpersonal problems.
- If child sexual abuse is not reported then the same abuser may harm other children or may target the same child again.
- There is very often a pattern to abuser's behaviour. They usually repeat their behaviour and with many children as well.
- Children of any age can be abused. Reported incidents show that even infants have been sexually abused. (Tulir, 2011)

These analytical findings make use of a slightly variant definition of the term 'child', as an individual below eighteen is conceived as one who will not lie or weave stories of sexual abuse. The findings explain why the perpetrators cannot be said to belong to any particular age group; nor could they be categorized as belonging to any one social class (except in some extraordinary cases) or ethnic group. Gender is also not a limiting factor, as women too, although not in great numbers, abuse children even sexually. However, according to the present study significant one-third of the offenders are senior children. It is to be noted that not only do children in their teens sexually abuse other children, they even commit planned rape (in the middle of May, 2012, a ninth class student, belonging to Thiruvananthapuram, took a mentally retarded young woman to the local cinema as if to show her a movie and raped her in the bathroom) and murder (again in May 2012 a fifteen-year-old ninth class student in Pathanamthitta District murdered his classmate in cold blood, in retaliation to a petty offence committed by the dead child an year ago). All of them perpetrators exploit the trust, the inability to resist, and weakness of their victim.

Availability of Child Abuse Data in the State

Collecting data from the state was difficult. The NGO Childline is a national reporting agency which started functioning only in 1996, started its offices in Kerala in association with the social services department very late, that too in nine out of the fourteen districts. Their data bank has a confusing array of details which a researcher cannot easily avail. Jananeethi, a registered NGO operating in Thrissur District from 1992 began considering the problem only by 2006. NGO services are new and limited. Not much of them function in the field of child abuse. In fact child abuse has caught the attention of the media only after cases of abuse in the tourism centres, predominantly in Kovalam and Kumarakom caught the attention of the Press as places where sexual abuse of children happen. The first Annotated bibliography of child abuse (Bhan 1990) gives short accounts of what happened mainly in the West and the USA. Child Abuse as a problem worthy of attention was comparatively unknown to the populace in this part of the country till the last decade of the twentieth century. In 2003 a Tourism related project was undertaken by Equations. In 2004, ICDS (Integrated Child Development Services), which functions under the Department of Social Welfare conducted a survey on child abuse in all of its projects and circulated the report among the LSGs for intervention. In 2004 the SWD approached the Home Department for revitalising the functioning of district level Juvenile Police Units, which indicates that the units were not functioning when the report was given. In 2007 the report by the MWCD collected data for the entire state from two districts, Ernakulam and Wyanad.

The official website of the Department of Social Services, Government of Kerala, active since 2011, declares:

> But there are areas still we have to reach out.... In the case of children above 6 years the issues are in the form of dropouts from schools, child abuse, adolescent issues, HIV infection, child labour, illegal child trafficking, street children, children with disabilities and those in difficult circumstances, etc.

This is the official admission of the fact the child abuse and child trafficking were and are a reality the magnitude of which remains to be measured.

The survey of the Social Service Department (2005) conducted among students between the age of 14 and 18 prompted the Government to go into the deeper levels of the problem. (How far did they go wasn't known at the time of preparing this report?) The survey found that a large number of the students were victims of emotional and physical abuse.

At least 24 per cent of the students, who answered the survey for gauging the extent and nature of child abuse in Kerala, indicated that they were fed up with life, which is an early symptomatic exposition of suicide urge. 22 per cent of the respondents said they had been ridiculed in the name of caste, family status or physical disability. 24 per cent revealed that they had endured instances of "uneasiness" when persons touched them without reason, an answer which was described as indicative of the prevalence of sexual abuse of children. 9.5 per cent of the children had to work outside home for "wages or food". 40 per cent reported harsh punishment at home, including inflicting of minor burns and being tied up. 68 per cent of the respondents faced "punishment and blame from parents and teachers" for not scoring marks to their expectations. A bigger majority (71 per cent) constantly endured reprimand at home. 30 per cent of the children felt "neglected". 7 per cent, including girls (1 per cent) had been "prompted" to use beedi, alcohol, panmasala and cigarettes. The SWD categorised 4.7 per cent of the respondents as victims of family conflict and 10.8 per cent as victims of abuse by relatives.

It has come to the notice of this researcher that in Kerala some people who have for long remained socially and economically weak have due to ignorance and deprivation entered into practices of child sexual abuse. Among certain communites sodomy appears to be a tradition. Two NGOs in Kannur and Kasargod—Jeevansamskriti and NYK have unofficially confirmed that hundreds of school boys who were mutually abusive had approached them for advise on how to prevent AIDS. These were homosexuals below eighteen who were also victims of pedophilia. To assess the magnitude of the problem during the focal period this researcher requested NYK Kasaragod, to provide the number of homosexuals who they call MSM, of the age group 18 to 21—since they have not recorded the younger visitors—who have registered with them. The number given from Neeleswaram block alone was 539; because they said they didn't have the record of the entire district. If the official figure could be so high in a single block, the situation in the entire district is well within comprehension.

The number of school children abused by a single individual and the number of repeated events, especially from Malappuram and Kasaragod indicates the level of vulnerability. A large scale abuse of school children is possible and only later will the incident come to the notice of the concerned. The vulnerability is enhanced by the general feeling created by the visual media and careless parents.

Disappearance/missing of children is a problem the causes of which are on the one hand poverty and deprivation (Justice Gafoor 2010) and on the other all the evils of abuse discussed earlier. Child trafficking which is the result of all the above and mafia activities is of great threat to the state.

Kerala state crime records bureau does not consider child labour as a case of criminal nature. The department of labour has noted only a negligible number of instances of child labour in the State that too of children brought from other states. However, the present study is able to identify that open and hidden child labour are rampant in the state. Children from the low income families in the state are attracted to work that bring them money.

Selective Neglect in the State

Traditionally boys who were considered to be the future providers of the family received more attention than girls and children who were invalid. Parents of girls are required to spend much energy in finding a husband, a great amount of money to send a daughter in marriage, and in certain communities like the Nairs, even care for their children. Thus a girl child is a drain on the family's resources. It has therefore been the practice to feed the male children better and give them better education. This tendency is gradually changing as more and more females are becoming wage earners and therefore providers. In the present state survival rates for boys in Kerala differ from the rest of India. According to 2001 census reports on Kerala, for 1000 males there were 1058 females (National average, 933). In 2011 the provisional data shows an increase, 1084 females for 1000 males (National average, 940). This advantage is an indicator of more female survival.

Child sex ratio for 2001 (0 to 6 years): 96.2 girls for 100 boys

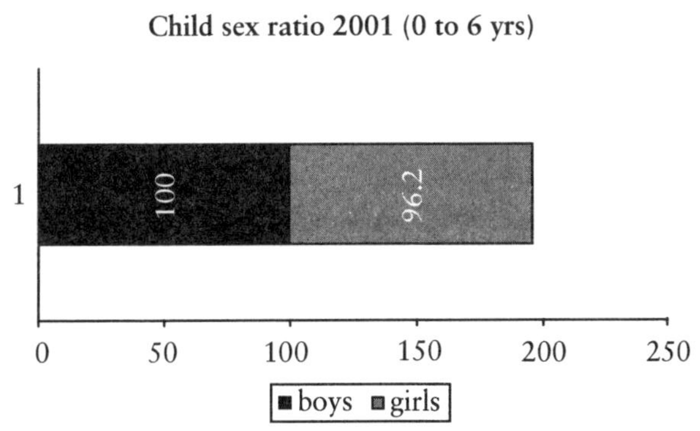

Total child population (0–6 yrs.) of Kerala in 2011: 33,22,247 (census report 2011)

Child Population of Kerala in 2011

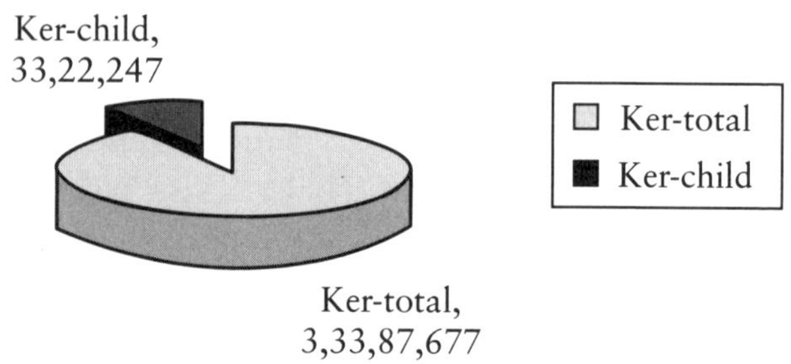

Child Population: Male-Female

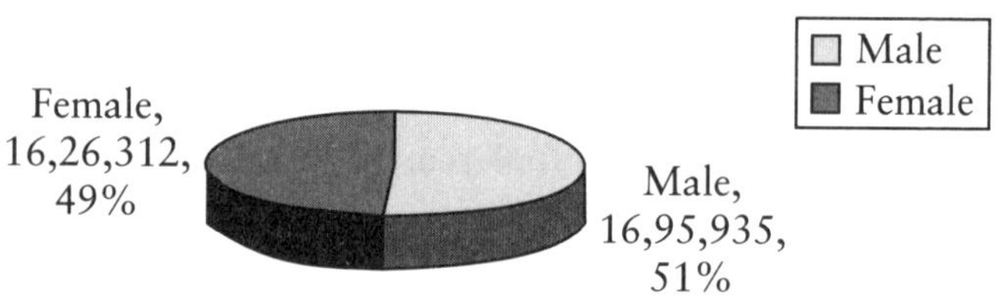

Literacy Rate—National and Kerala

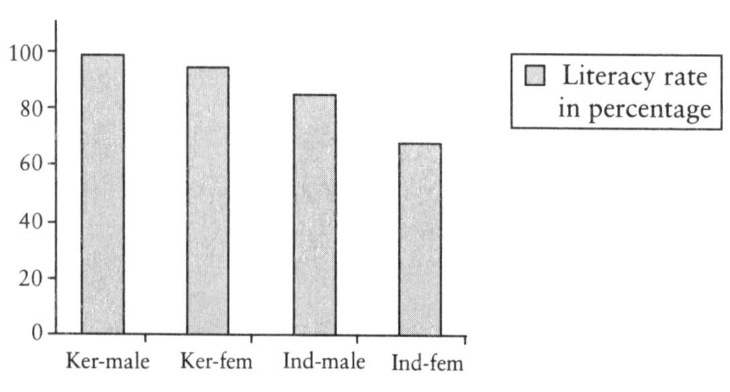

Kerala Literacy-district wise percetage

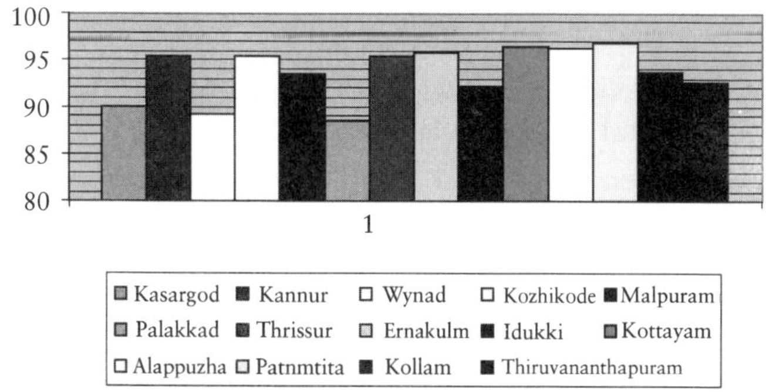

Kasaragod	89.95
Kannur	95.41
Wynad	89.32
Kozhikode	95.34
Malappuram	93.55
Palakkad	88.49
Thrissur	95.32
Ernakulam	95.68
Idukki	92.3
Kottayam	96.4
Alappuzha	96.26
Pathanamthitta	96.93
Kollam	93.77
Thiruvananthapuram	92.66

Literacy rate in Kerala is well above the National rate with the highest in Pathanamthitta (96.93) and lowest in Palakkad (88.49).

Accoridng to UNICEF Annual Report for 2010:

- Over 27 million births are recorded in India every year.
- The number of children under 18 is 424 million which comprises 37 per cent of the overall population.

- The population of children below 18 years in Uttar Pradesh alone is equal to the total child population of the United States of America.
- Child population (Below 18 years) of Kerala is equal to the total child population of Italy (UNICEF, 2008).
- Between 2000 and 2009, India has registered an impressive economic growth rate of around 7 per cent. Yet 37 per cent of the population lives below the official poverty line.
- Forty-two per cent of the rural people and 26 per cent of the urban people are below the official poverty line (Press Release of Central statistics office 2010).
- Infant mortality rate is the highest in Madhya Pradesh (70/1000) and the lowest in Kerala (12/1000).

  (SRS Bulletin, Vol. 44, No. 1, Oct. 2009)

There are 33,22,247 children below the age of six in the State as per Census 2011 provisional figures. They constitute 9.95 per cent of the state's population. The total number of children below 18 according to the State Census Director's letter on 4-3-2011 was 1,00,09,769. This figure is used for analysis of data in the later chapters.

Measures to Protect Child Rights

3

UN

A child is defined by the Convention on the Rights of the Child (CRC) as "Every human being below the age of 18 years unless under the law applicable under the child majority is attained earlier." The harshness of child abuse is implied in the WHO's definition of the problem.

Child Abuse: Definition

Child abuse or maltreatment constitutes all forms of physical and/or emotional ill-treatment, sexual abuse, neglect or negligent treatment or commercial or other exploitation, resulting in actual or potential harm to the child's health, survival, development or dignity in the context of a relationship of responsibility, trust or power.

Physical abuse of a child is that which results in actual or potential physical harm from an interaction or lack of an interaction, which is reasonably within the control of a parent or person in a position of responsibility, power or trust. There may be a single or repeated incidents.

Emotional abuse includes the failure to provide a developmentally appropriate, supportive environment, including the availability of a primary attachment figure, so that the child can develop a stable and full range of emotional and social competencies commensurate with her or his personal potentials and in the context of the society in which the child dwells. There may also be acts towards the child that cause or have a high probability of causing harm to the child's health or physical, mental, spiritual, moral or social development. These acts must be reasonably within the control of the parent or person in a relationship of responsibility, trust or power. Acts include restriction of movement, patterns of belittling, denigrating, scapegoating, threatening, scaring, discriminating, ridiculing or other non-physical forms of hostile or rejecting treatment.

Neglect is the failure to provide for the development of the child in all spheres: health, education, emotional development, nutrition, shelter, and safe living conditions, in the context of resources reasonably available to the family or caretakers and causes or has a high probability of causing harm to the child's health or physical, mental, spiritual, moral or social development. This includes the failure to properly supervise and protect children from harm as much as is feasible.

Child sexual abuse is the involvement of a child in sexual activity that he or she does not fully comprehend, is unable to give informed consent to, or for which the child is not developmentally prepared and cannot give consent, or that violates the laws or social taboos of society. Child sexual abuse is evidenced by this activity between a child and an adult or another child who by age or development is in a relationship of responsibility, trust or power, the activity being intended to gratify or satisfy the needs of the other person. This may include but is not limited to:

- The inducement or coercion of a child to engage in any unlawful sexual activity.
- The exploitative use of child in prostitution or other unlawful sexual practices.
- The exploitative use of children in pornographic performances and materials.

Exploitation

Commercial or other exploitation of a child refers to use of the child in work or other activities for the benefit of others. This includes, but is not limited to, child labour and child prostitution. These activities are to the detriment of the child's physical or mental health, education, or spiritual, moral or social-emotional development.

Source: pp. 13-17, Report of the Consultation on Child Abuse Prevention, Geneva, 29-31 March 1999, World Health Organization, Social Change and Mental Health, Violence and Injury Prevention.

The UN Declaration of the Rights of the Child in 1959 is a milestone in the history of child welfare. In 1989 the UN General Assembly adopted the Convention on the Rights of the Child. Majority of the member countries including India ratified the convention. The convention outlined the fundamental rights of children—they possessed the right to be protected

- from economic exploitation
- from harmful work
- from physical or mental violence
- from sexual exploitation and abuse
- from separation from their families against their will

It has been internationally agreed that violation of the rights of the child to exist as a free, safe and happy individual is a global phenomenon. Therefore the United Nations Convention on the Rights of the Child (UNCRC) decrees that minimum entitlements and freedoms should be afforded to all persons below the age of 18 regardless of race, colour, gender, language, religion, opinions, origins, wealth, birth status or ability and therefore apply to all people everywhere. The UN finds these rights interdependent and indivisible, meaning that a right cannot be fulfilled at the expense of another right.

The purpose of the UNCRC is to outline the basic human rights that should be afforded to children. There are four broad classifications of these rights. These four categories cover all civil, political, social, economic and cultural rights of every child.

- **Right to Survival:** A child's right to survival begins before a child is born. According to Government of India, a child's life begins after twenty weeks of conception. Hence the right to survival is inclusive of the child's rights to be born, right to minimum standards of food, shelter and clothing, and the right to live with dignity.

- **Right to Protection:** A child has the right to be protected from neglect, exploitation and abuse at home, and elsewhere.
- **Right to Participation:** A child has a right to participate in any decision-making that involves him/her directly or indirectly. There are varying degrees of participation as per the age and maturity of the child.
- **Right to Development:** Children have the right to all forms of development: Emotional, Mental and Physical. Emotional development is fulfilled by proper care and love of a support system, mental development through education and learning and physical development through recreation, play and nutrition.

This follows that according to UN, when anyone or more than one, or all of these rights are violated, that becomes child abuse and whoever does that is the abuser.

India

For the first time in India severity of child abuse and the threats to childhood were brought out by a government sponsored study in 2007. The findings indicate that abuse of all forms are rampant in the country.

424 million individuals below 18 live in India. This is 37 per cent of the total population of India (UNICEF 2010) (Census 2011 is expected to provide the latest figures). According to the study cited, more than 70 per cent of the children in India are physically abused which has serious impacts on their physical and emotional growth. More than 53 per cent of the children are sexually abused, and a 50 per cent suffer emotional abuse. This is a rate which is surprisingly high and indicates how unsafe childhood in India is. This alarming state of affairs suggests that India with its 'synthetic culture and perfumes of tolerance and patience' is not behind any third world country in abusive behaviour towards children. Perhaps in the past it wasn't as much severe.

A number of legislations have been introduced time to time to protect child rights, in recognition of the fact that child abuse is a reality which needs combat. The measures suggested by UN to contain child abuse at the global level have been ratified by India.

The Constitution of India on the Rights of the Child

The Constitution of India has in its articles decreed that the States have power to evolve measures for the protection and care of children.

Article 15(3) states that nothing in this article shall prevent the state from making any special provision for women and children.

Article 21A assures free and compulsory education for all children between 6 and 14 years.

According to article 24 no child below the age of fourteen shall be employed to work in any factory or mine or engaged in any other hazardous employment.

Article 39 makes it explicit that the States shall make sure that the tender age of children is not abused and that they are given opportunities and facilities to develop in a healthy manner and in conditions of freedom and dignity and that childhood and youth are protected against moral and material abandonment.

POLICIES AND LEGISLATIONS IN INDIA

National Policy for Children 1974

Policy measures adopted by the Government of India's National Policy for Children 1974 item (viii) states that delinquents and begging children shall be rehabilitated, (ix) states that children shall be protected against neglect, cruelty and exploitation and (x) says that no child under 14 shall be permitted to be engaged in hazardous occupation. This policy does speak about abuse indirectly but does not define the problem. Thus the national policy of 1974 does not identify the existence of a problem called child abuse.

National Charter for Children 2004

National charter for children 2004 is the result of the increasing awareness that a healthy childhood is important to the nation. The Charter speaks about the need for social protection of children, and doles out measures to eliminate threats to children's survival and liberty. It recognizes the need to create an exploitation free environment that safeguards the child from abuse with special emphasis on the girl child. Children of the marginalized and disadvantaged communities who are more vulnerable to exploitation of all kind have to be given extra care and protection. Procedures that are child friendly have to be adopted.

National Plan of Action for Children 2005 is a construct of the Ministry of Women and Child Development which aims at the execution of what was envisioned in the National Charter 2004. It declares the child as an asset of the nation. It wants to address all issues that batter a child's growth, like inequality, discrimination or deprivation. The most dispossessed among the children will receive benefit out of its proceedings. A comprehensive study of childhood and the problems children face during the different phases of growth in order to evolve equitable solutions is an important objective of NPAC.

Immoral Traffic (Prevention) Act, 1956 and Immoral Traffic (Prevention) Amendment Bill 2006, determine the child as a person who has not completed 16 years. This was intended to prevent the sexual exploitation or abuse of persons for commercial purposes or for consideration of money or in any other kind.

The Government of India enacted the Juvenile Justice (Care and Protection of Children) Act in 2000. This legislation ensures protection to children in need of care, and juvenile offenders. The provisions under this act are set according to the UN Convention on the Rights of the Child. In this act a child or juvenile is defined as a person who has not completed his/her 18th year of age. According to this act, if a crime or an incident of that nature took place while the person was a child, and then during the proceedings the juvenile ceased to be of age, the case would continue as if the juvenile has not turned eighteen yet. The second chapter of the Act addresses Juveniles in Conflict with Law (JCLs). This section calls for the establishment of

Juvenile Justice Boards (JJBs) where the State Government sees fit.

The Commission for Protection of Child Rights Act, 2005, was for the protection of Child Rights and setting up Children's Courts for providing speedy trial of offences against children or of violation of child Rights. This document states that India is committed to UN declaration on Survival, Protection and Development of children. India has also acceded to the Convention on the Rights of the Child (CRC), which is an international treaty. The country is bound to uphold the treaty, in consequence of which India has adopted National Charter for Children, 2003. The UN General Assembly Special Session of Children, held in May 2002, adopted an outcome document titled a "World Fit for Children" containing goals, objectives, and strategies to be undertaken by the member countries. The CPCR 2005 was amended in 2006. Rules for the commission were set in the same year (2006). The act initiates provisions for setting up commissions for the protection of child rights at the central and state level with powers to evolve measures to safeguard every right of every child.

The Right of Children to Free and Compulsory Education Act, 2009

The UN Convention on Rights of the Child which India ratified puts any form of suppression of the child's right to a decent living as an infringement that is punishable. Child labour takes away the kind of life the child is entitled to lead and is therefore a vitiation of the rights. The Right of Children to Free and Compulsory Education Act, 2009, of the Ministry of Law and Justice, which defines child as a male or female of the age six to fourteen, states that all children in the country between the age group specified shall receive compulsory education. When basic education is compulsory, the state is bound to provide schooling facilities to all and the parents and caretakers are bound to educate their children. The Act can through its impact save childhood from abuse, thereby save many buds of promise. Protocol on Prevention, Rescue, Repatriation and Rehabilitation of Trafficked and Migrant

Child Labour (2008) of the Ministry of Labour and Employment rectifies some of the loopholes of Child Labour (Prohibition and Regulation) Act 1986 and Juvenile Justice Act 2000.

Although many legal measures of protection have been adopted by the Government, the actual situation is far from desirable.

According to the critics of the Right to Education Act (RTE Act), it is designed to sustain a discriminatory multi-layered school system and thereby accelerate both commoditization of school education, on the one hand and exclusion of the poor, on the other. This will become a major obstacle in the much desired and talked about child friendly transformation. It has been observed that those prepared the blue print of the Act, therefore, have been acting as agents of the neo-liberal capital than as the guardian of the people's democratic rights to equitable development and welfare guaranteed in the Constitution (Sadgopal 2011).

Spread of self-financing institutions and the government policy of lip service are a great hindrance to proper growth through education. Of late, the government has become less serious about the education of the children of the poor people. Problems like child labour, lack of physical and academic infrastructure in school, the issue of good quality education, availability of schools within the reach of children, education of children with disabilities, among other things have not yet been addressed despite enactment of the law. Inaction on the part of the executive to perform its constitutional and statutory duties forces social workers to resort to avoidable litigations (Asok Agarwal 2011). Thus, according to its critics the RTE Act itself is a violation of child rights.

The Protection of Children from Sexual Offences, Bill 2011, which is an improvised form of The Offences Against Children (Prevention) Bill 2005, defines child as "any person below the age of eighteen years save as provided otherwise".

The Bill is the latest among the several bills passed by the Indian Parliament to safeguard the interests of the country's children. This proposes stringent punishment for offences of sexual assault on children, child harassment and child pornography.

The Bill treats child sexual abuse as "aggravated offence" when a person who is responsible for his/her protection or who the child trusts, commits the offence. It also considers the physical/mental disability and the long-term after-effects of the injury inflicted. The perpetrators of pornographic abuse of children and even those who possess such material are punishable. Designated special courts will decide cases in a time-bound manner. The bill outlines the various procedures of investigation, trial and sensitive dispensation of justice. It sets guidelines for media to sensitively and discreetly report cases without inflicting pain of identification of the victim.

The protection of children from sexual abuse Bill, 2011, is an attempt to modify the existing penalties for the offenders by specifying various forms of abuse against boys and girls below eighteen. The contention that boys are not sexually abused is re-written in the 2011 bill, as it was revealed in the 2007 Report on Child Abuse (Ministry of Women and Children) that places more boys in the vulnerable category.

The Bill, like the earlier Bills on children, aims at the welfare of the children of the country. However, without a strong will to enforce it the bill would remain like the rest of those bills without results.

The social welfare department of the Government of India, in their National Policy for Children, August 1974 states that the children are a supremely important asset, whose nurture and solicitude are the nation's responsibility. The policy stresses on children's programmes that find prominent part in the national development of human resources so that the children grow up to become robust citizens, physically fit, mentally alert and morally healthy, endowed with skills and motivations provided by the society. The policy measures ensure the safety of children from neglect and torture and affirms the need for free and compulsory education for all children up to the age of fourteen. This rhetoric has been repeated in all subsequent governmental proclamations regarding the welfare of children.

Thirty years later the report on child abuse in India by the Ministry of Women and Children comes out with statistics of the woes of children in India. The report indicates that despite several measures the children face severe problems ranging from familial ones to those from the wider realms of the society which include the body of the market. And in 2011 the critics of the national government's attitude to children blame them of having no sincere wish to create an egalitarian and enlightened society through its children. The critics argue that the education system of the country of the day is neo-liberal, its core idea being opening new markets by demolishing the vast governmental school system. Pursuit of privatization and commercialization of education is another feature of neo-liberal education upheld by RTE Act (Anil Sadgopal 2011:8).

Why do Policies Become Less Effective?

Policies adopted by the government from time to time to improve the lot of the children are less effective because of the inherent defects. And the defects could be traced back to the wider larger corruption that Indians have gradually accepted as part of life. What is called globalization has legalized this entry into corruption.

> ...the relationship inherent in globalization is not based on equality, as the term seems to suggest, but on domination and subordination. The process by which both domination and subordination are brought into being are extremely complex in nature. They involve political influence, economic control, and the cultural presence of the globalizing forces which affects the identity of the nation. As a consequence, the way a nation looks up on itself begins to change. Colonial rulers, following their ideologue James Mill, propagated the idea that Indians were immoral, corrupt and devious people, which eventually Indians themselves started to believe and they have now taken to practising it as well,... (K.N. Panikkar 2011:102).

The beneficiaries of globalization in every field have started looking at the operations of the global capital as a chance for modernization, even at greater loss to the common people. Resistance to this sort of colonization has begun, but hasn't yet caught momentum, as cultural colonization which is intense and widespread has already taken the lead. Culture plays vital role in the making of a nation. For policies to become effective strengthening collective will which is beyond rhetoric is necessary. Social scientists like K.N. Panicker believe that revitalizing and integrating Indian culture can retain human qualities of the people, and enable them to work out their own way (Panicker 2011). The children need good adult models to develop human qualities. This is a difficult, but practical way out of the situation.

Methodology

4

The methodology adopted is one that can gauge the dimensions of child abuse in the state. Although the Department of Social Welfare has conducted research on abuse among the school children of the state (2005) there was no study that could serve as a model for the present researcher to adopt. The report by the Ministry of Women and Child Development (2007) was there. The sample design of the present study is not an extension of the one used in the MWCD report. The definition of child abuse in the present study should suit the distinctive context of the society of Kerala which in a good many ways is different from the rest of India. Therefore the definition of the term child abuse has to receive special attention. In this chapter the design and methodology of the study is delineated.

Objectives

The main objective of the project is to conduct a comprehensive study of the problem of child abuse in Kerala through an inquiry into the state of affairs of children in the State.

This shall attempt to uncover the magnitude of the problem through an assessment of the circumstances and investigation of the causes. It shall bring out why the problem deserves urgent attention.

Definition of the Term 'Child'

For the purpose of this study 'child' is defined as any person below the age of eighteen.

Definition of Child Abuse

Child abuse is any act of commission or omission by individuals, institutions or society as a whole, and any conditions resulting from such acts or inactions, which deprive children of their equal rights and liberties and/or interfere with their optimal development, constitute by definition abusive or neglectful acts or conditions.

Design of the Study

The study is based on the assumption that in the State there is high incidence of child abuse of different types. The study attempts to assess the magnitude of child abuse during the period of study. The picture brought forth is one that was obtained during the course of the survey. The fact that during the term of this project the media, different social service organizations and the government have become alert on the subject is taken note of. Unlike in the case with countries like the USA, there is no data bank of child abuse available neither at the state level nor at the national level. The Head, South Regional Resource Centre of Child Line that keeps track of child maltreatment telephonically, admits that the NGO doesn't operate in every district of Kerala and that the telephonically received complaints of child abuse are very bulky and not easily manageable.

> Childline is not functioning in Kollam, Pathanamthitta, and Alappuzha. Also some of the Childlines are not yet 5 years old therefore information will not be available for these categories for the period of time requested.... Since the information sought involves 1000s to lakhs (in the case of emotional abuse) of cases this is practically impossible to attempt. (*Source*: Letter from the Head, South Regional Resource Centre, Childline India Foundation, Chennai, dated 28 March 2011.)

Therefore the study could not rely on such agencies for data. No proper official statistics that gave an exact picture of the problem was available. And for this reason data that lay outside the compass of such agencies was also sought.

Since the study was done by one who was not a trained social scientist, and since this was an area where economic factors interlaced with sociological, cultural, and psychological factors, the method might reveal a commonsensical critical approach to that segment of everyday reality which has to do with child abuse in Kerala rather than pure scientific analysis.

Coverage

For the enhancement of this study the investigator has encountered maximum possible number of child respondents from the districts in the north, south, and centre of the state.

From the north: Kasaragod, Kannur, Kozhikode, Malappuram and Palakkad;

From the centre: Thrissur and Ernakulam;

From the south: Kottayam, Pathanamthitta, Kollam and Thiruvanathapuram.

The number of samples was just as much as was necessary and there were limitations such as confidentiality and privacy of the children and families. There were also limitations to maintaining accuracy as all the children interviewed need not have given correct answers.

The police, the social welfare department, juvenile homes and the health department are the government agencies that have knowledge of different kinds of child maltreatment. Under the existing laws regarding child welfare, dealt with earlier in this study, these departments have roles and responsibilities in matters related to delinquency, domestic violence, felonious assault and homicide. The Childline is a government agency that keeps telephone (1098) alive for twenty-four hours to attend maltreatment issues. School teachers, private social service organizations, NGOs and those who run poor homes come under another category who know facts about child abuse. Some individuals like a parent, or relative or friend or neighbour may also have knowledge of what is happening about certain child. But a great number of incidents of abuse pass on without coming under anybody's notice. (The victims who say he or she hasn't disclosed the matter to anybody finally admit that.) But some children who never would want to disclose what happened might respond positively to tricky questions given to them in a questionnaire.

The teachers, the hospital and the psychologists might know incidents of abuse that the police and court would never know. Not every case reaches the legal authorities. Due to a number of reasons, the school, the psychiatrist and the psychologist, and the social workers do not report issues to the police. And the police too hush up some instances. This might affect the data whatsoever available with the government agencies. There are clear instructions in the various Acts concerning children as to the nature of maltreatment that should be reported. However the teacher, the psychologist or the psychiatrist might consider his/her advice more beneficial to the child than the proceedings of the court. In the recent past in the northern districts of Kerala there were instances of intervention by Childline when school authorities brought large scale incidents of abuse to their notice.

Respondents

Children between 10 and 18 years

Young adults

Parents, teachers, police, doctors and other adults who could provide useful information

Sample Size

3210 children from 11 districts (against a target of 3300)

The state being a narrow stretch of land from north to south it is not difficult to divide Kerala into zones for collecting representative samples. For this purpose the State has been taken as three zones, viz., the south, the centre, and the north. Samples from the south were collected from Thiruvananthapuram, Kollam, Pathanamthitta and Kottayam. The districts of Ernakulam and Thrissur in the central zone, Palakkad, Malappuram, Kozhikode, Kannur and Kasaragod in the north. In sample collection whether or not to include a child belonging to a particular community, Adivasi for example, wasn't the concern. No deliberate attempt was made to include or exclude a particular community.

Tools for Research

Confidential questionnaire.

One to one interaction to elicit specific information.

Theme Centred Interaction to establish rapport with the children and enable them to open up.

Ethical guidelines for the researcher, so that the process of collecting data shall not upset children.

Where it Happens?

Abuse might happen in the victim's own house, a relative's house, a neighbour's house, a friend's house, at school, at the place where the child is employed as a wage earner or domestic help, religious schools, house boats, beauty parlours, ice cream parlours, poor homes/home for destitute children and clinics where anesthetics are used in treatment. In the case of some victims the person who first comes to know the event of abuse may be a neighbour, or a member of the victim's family or a teacher. They may talk about the incident but may not be interested in going ahead with other measures which are practically not known to them. Or they may habitually attach nothing more than gossip value to the event. But this is not always the case. They, especially the teachers, may also take up the matter with the police.

There are children who do not possess the discriminatory capacity or awareness to understand that they are being abused. They are given to believe that what is happening is nothing unusual. Abusive behaviour of the sexual kind happen even at some centres that supposedly impart religious lessons (cf. Pallath 2004), and at homes for destitutes. Children at day care centres are victims to maltreatment by caretakers. In the hostels they are maltreated by the owner and some of the employees.

Some children who are socially deficient are incapable of understanding that they are under abuse. (The case of a community in the north of Kerala referred to earlier in the study is a case in point.) This abuse is not easily recognized.

In a situation where there is no system that maintains the record of all the abused children in anyone district or state, a data bank is unthinkable. The researcher, therefore, met children in person to take their responses, apart from meeting stake holders and NGOs to draw together their views. Reports in the daily newspapers, interviews in the TV channels that appeared during the time of study, expository essays by individuals in magazines and internet sources also have served as data providers.

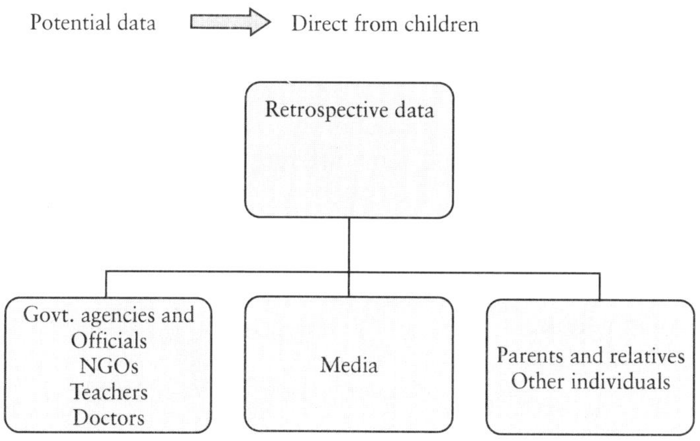

Although it could be the tip of an ice berg and insufficient for an in-depth study, account on children who have undergone abuse available with police, social service department, health department and govt. instituted NGOs constituted minimal retrospective data. Potential data was collected by the investigator through meetings with children. Since in Kerala most children attend schools, the schools are an appropriate place to locate them in large numbers. Therefore meetings with children in schools in the state were arranged with prior permission from the Director of Public Instructions, Government of Kerala. The investigator with the help of other assisting personnel prepared questionnaires, which could extract trustworthy information from children, young adults, and adults.

Period of Study

The period of this study was from February 2009 to July 2011.

During the first half of this period, background work like collection of secondary data was done. The time allocated for collection of data from the field was a period of 12 months between Jan. 2010 and Jan. 2011. The number of maltreated children was collected during this period, but in different stages. In the districts selected survey was conducted at different spots at different times. The data thus obtained was supplemented by the data taken from other sources.

Typology of Abuse

In order to arrive at a definition of child abuse, typology has been framed based on different abusive/maltreatment situations.

Physical abuse

Beating

Thrashing

Slap on the face

Pulling by hair

Kicking and punching

Burns and cuts

Emotional abuse

Frequent accusations

Frequent insults

Use of abusive language

Terrorising

Threats of sexual abuse

Calling the child a nuisance and a burden

Creating low esteem

Cheating the child with offers

Making the child eat leftover food

Child labour

Labour due to circumstances

Child working as domestic help

Child working in hotel, resort/houseboat

Child working as construction helper

Agricultural helper

Sex abuse

Forcing into sodomy and other unnatural sex acts

Early introduction into sexuality through coaxing and bullying

Using mobile phone porno to induce a child into sexuality

Trapping or inducing into sex acts through internet chat

Seducing a child through mobile phone SMS

'Sodomising' the child after intoxicating him

Showing porn pictures and other sexually explicit materials

Offering money and sweets to sexually trap children

Offering employment to traffic children

Note: In districts like Kasaragod and Malappuram abuse of male children by adult males and other male children is conceived by certain section of the population in that region as a common everyday event. This willed ignorance on the part of parents is reckoned as sexual abuse in this study.

Substance abuse

Intoxicating the child with alcohol

Selling drugs to the child

Offering the child alcohol

Offering narcotics

Tempting the child to chew drugged pan-masala

Selling drugged ice-cream to the child

Offering cigarettes

Consuming alcohol in the presence of the child

Neglect

Exposure to inciting behaviours and unhealthy inducement by television channels

Allowing unsupervised use of internet and cell phone

Leaving to physically and emotionally unsafe environment

Not providing opportunities to learn/causing hindrance to education

Data Collection

For data collection the study used reference period of one year from Jan. 2010 to Jan. 2011. During this period the investigator traveled in the districts in the zones selected for study and with the help of resource persons available in the immediate environment, collected data from children, young adults and adults. The investigator was aware that researchers were not known to have handled the problem extensively in the state. So the motto of this study was to find the uninvestigated children and bring out the hitherto uninvestigated dimensions of the problem.

Media reports on abuse were utilized in order to augment the interpretability of the findings. The directly observed facts were thus supplemented by this data.

In the first stage of sampling, the regions of the districts selected have been distinguished into rural and urban as per the intensity of urbanization; for example, although administration-wise Kazhakkoottam is part of Thiruvanathapuram corporation there is difference in the degree of urbanization. There are also differences between the socio-attitudinal functions and behaviour of people belonging to two rural areas in two districts. For example the people of Neeleswaram or Kumbala in Kasaragod district may exhibit an attitude to children which is different from what is experienced by the children belonging to the village of Kadachira in the neighbouring district of Kannur. However, studying distinction of this kind hasn't been the main concern.

How was Child Abuse Determined?

1. Respondents were below the age of 18 at the time of meeting.
2. The abuse happened at the respondents (victim's) home, or at school or workplace, in the neighbourhood or at a place known to the child.
3. The abuse was detrimental to the child's well-being.
4. There were minimum evidence necessary to call the act 'abuse' or 'maltreatment' or 'neglect'.
5. The abuser was an adult or one who was below 18 who could willfully assault the child.

Identifying Different Types of Abuse

Different types of abuse have been listed earlier. What all could be counted as sexual abuse and what all emotional abuse and neglect, etc. have been outlined. The typology of abuse determined, the responses received from the body of respondents could be put into one or other category. Neglect can happen only from a parent or an equally responsible person. Those families that live in insecure circumstances may unwittingly or out of helplessness neglect their children. Such a behaviour was not considered neglect. The person who neglects must be legally or morally responsible for the child's well-being and should intentionally abuse or neglect them. Food, clothes, shelter, medicine, education, physical and mental protection come under the responsibility of such persons.

Data Analysis

Data analysis includes finding out how many children out of totality were subject to different abuse in Kerala during the period of data collection. The samples represent the total child population of the State. The rate of each abuse among the samples therefore signify the rate of abuse of that type in the entire state.

As stated elsewhere in the study no popular statistical tool of measurement has been used. It however arrives at the estimated total of children below eighteen who were victims of various kinds of abuse in the state. Sometimes regional characteristics have to do with abuse of certain kind because the perpetrators of that kind of abuse are found mostly in that region. The state level estimate has been prepared out of the total samples.

Limitations

The study for the most part depended on the efforts of a single individual, the researcher (investigator).

A comprehensive study on child abuse in the State has not been attempted earlier. The study, being on a sensitive area with no data bank, had to rely on limited resources.

The tendency to abuse perceived in the State in the present times has no precise precedent.

A broad study of the causes of abuse is very complex and needs elaborate study design.

Accuracy of the information obtained from child respondents depended partly on how the questions were framed and partly on the nature of the child answering the questions.

An extensive work on the problem needs an extensive framework and resources to maintain high degree of accuracy in data collection.

An in-depth study of a problem of such magnitude requires strenuous data collection and detailed analysis. The present study being one conducted chiefly by a single person, therefore, has constraints.

5 Magnitude and Intensity of Child Abuse in Kerala

In this study the term abuse is used to mean all types of child abuse. The term child used with 'neglect' and 'labour' may not directly belong to the category of abuse but is in effect the result of a tendency to abuse because the result is detrimental to the growth of the child.

To whatever strata of the society the child belongs, the abused individual, the child, is a sufferer. In the context of the Kerala of the present, many things that happen around along with that attitude of the parents that lacks concern for the child have adverse impact on the child. This, according to the definition, is abuse. The neo-liberal economic order that dominates the nation's official attitude to everything has been effecting changes in the socio-cultural outlook of the people. The child that is exposed to neo-colonial culture may turn to look at his or her (even) caring parents as mere providers of facilities. On the contrary the parents and care-givers tend to look at their wards as mere commodities. This would mean that factors outside home have a very strong influence on the attitude that causes abuse.

The information on abuse that this report presents pertains to the different forms of abuse perpetrated/reported, during the period of study, based on the data collected state-wide during the span of one year. The estimated number of child abuse is what happened in the entire state, not in any single district or block. The number of abuse shown is children abused per cent which is representative of the total child population of the state unless otherwise stated. The period during which the investigator collected data from children in the state is the focal period. The information on abuse obtained from the child is the information that the child could let the investigator know, which has been happening, or which happened in the past which he or she could remember vividly. That means the event of abuse need not belong to the focal period. This, therefore, is the number of abuse prevailing at the time of data collection.

Assessing Abuse

When we examine abuse in the present context, it is worthwhile to consider similar studies conducted earlier by different agencies. This is helpful in assessing the present state of the problem. The present study also considers factors not taken up for consideration by others.

The estimate on child abuse in Kerala shown in the 2005 report of the Department of Social Welfare, Government of Kerala and 2007 report on child abuse by the Central Ministry of Women and Child Development are given after the data obtained during the present investigation. This would help demonstrate the direction of movement of abuse during the period after the earlier studies. Table 1 specifies the percentage of abuse out of the samples taken—3210 children out of the total child population (based on the data on child population available during the study). Table 1 shows how many became victims of abuse of each type. According to the present estimate 50.31 per cent of the representative children—the child respondents—reported one or other form of abuse. This means that every second child was abused in the state during the period of study.

Comparisons with 2005 study of the Social Welfare Department of Kerala (and also with the one conducted by the Ministry of Women and Child Development, 2007) indicated that abuse of all kinds were on the increase. There was (and is) an astonishing increase in sexual abuse in the state. This was indicative of the risk a child in Kerala had to confront in the social environment. The increase was significant during the extent of the study with a tendency to continue. This swell happened due to factors that might be open to analysis and controllable if the State has sufficient will power to empower the victim and restrain the perpetrator.

The exactness of the information on total population and the population of children in Kerala depended on the availability of data from the census department. Director of Census Operations, Kerala, on 4-3-2011 gave information on population of children below 18 years available to him on the that date. The population of children below 18 years in Kerala was 1,00,09,769 which was 2.37 per cent of the total child population of India. The latest position—according to census 2011—was not available at the time of preparing this report in the case of children below 18 years.

TABLE 1

Table indicating occurrence of abuse
Total number of Children below 18 surveyed: 3210

Type of abuse	Number of children reported abuse	% abused
Physical abuse	1424	44.36
Sexual abuse	1261	39.30
Emotional abuse	1829	59.00
Substance abuse	425	13.23
Total Neglect	1665	52.00

Occurrence of Abuse and Neglect

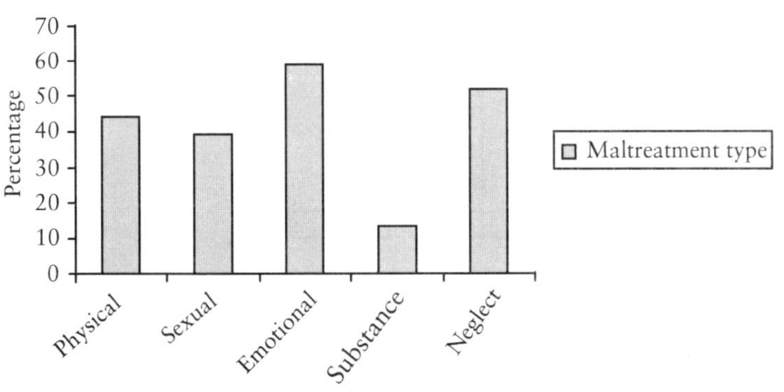

Occurrence of Abuse and Neglect

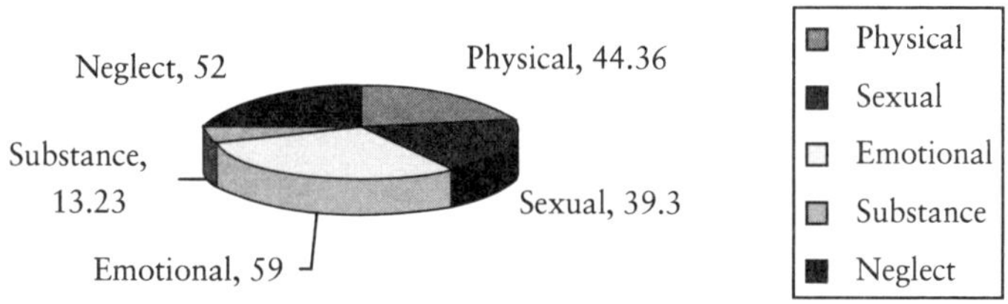

TABLE 2

Child Abuse in Kerala according to Department of Social Welfare, Government of Kerala, 2005

Percentage of children facing abuse

Type of abuse	Boys %	Girls %	Total %
Physical abuse	20	18.8	19.5
Sexual abuse	14.5	21	18
Substance abuse	10	2	6
Emotional abuse	54	57	56.6
Neglect	16	13	14.6

Child Abuse in Kerala acoording to Department of Social Welfare 2005

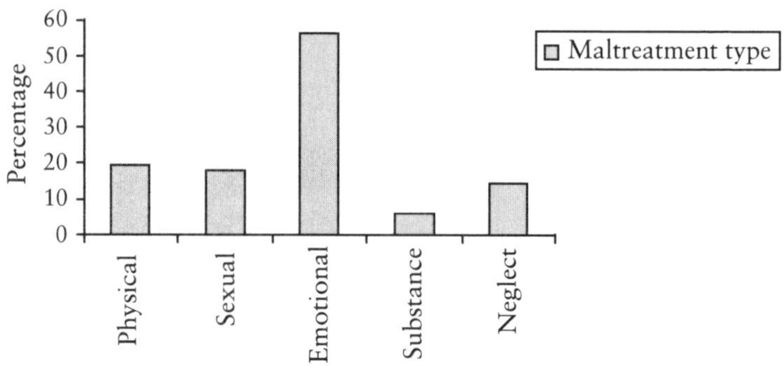

Abuse and Maltreatment (2005)

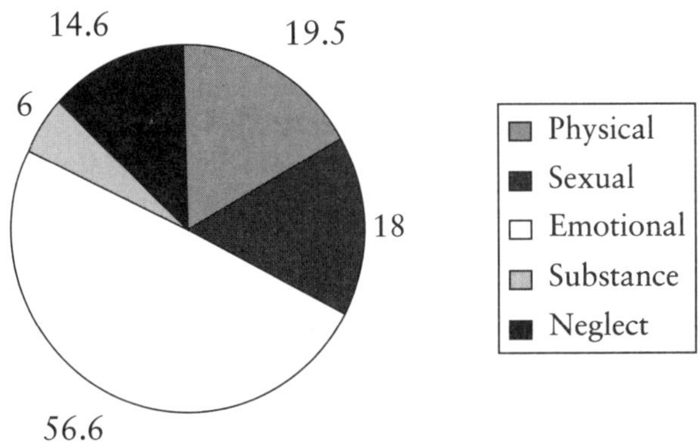

TABLE 3

Child Abuse in Kerala according to 2007 Report (MWCD)*

Percentage of children facing abuse

Type	Boys %	Girls %	Total %
Physical abuse	44.39	55.61	56.10
Sexual abuse	55.04	44.96	—
Emotional abuse	35.14	64.86	40.70
Substance abuse	—	—	—
Neglect (Girl child)			61.64

* Samples for this study were collected from two districts, Ernakulam and Wynad.

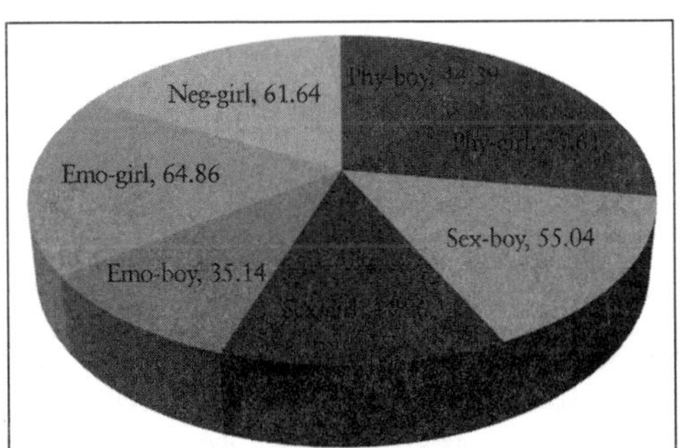

The first table which is according to the present findings indicates the occurrence of each kind of abuse out of the total samples. 44.36 per cent of the interviewed children reported physical abuse, 39.30 per cent were sexually abused, 59 per cent emotional abuse and 13.23 per cent reported substance abuse. 52 per cent reported neglect of all kind. The study conducted by the Department of Social Welfare of the Government of Kerala presented survey reports which showed occurrence of 19.5 per cent of physical abuse, 18 per cent sexual abuse, 56.6 per cent emotional abuse, 6 per cent substance abuse and 14.6 per cent of neglect. The report of MWCD showed much higher incidence rates. The difference between the findings of the present study and the study of 2005 was significant. Over the years there was 24.86 per cent increase in physical abuse, 21.30 per cent increase in sexual abuse, 7.23 per cent increase in substance abuse and emotional abuse has stepped up by 2.40 per cent. The increase in neglect, which was by 37.40 per cent, was substantial.

This is a pointer to the fact that abuse rate has increased significantly over the years. There is no corresponding increase in the total population of children in the State. In fact through the decade 2001–2011 the total number of children below six years has gone down by 470899, suggesting significant decline in birth rate. According to 2001 census, 11.9 per cent of the total population of Kerala was children up the age of six, whereas in 2011 it was only 10 per cent, which suggests the magnitude of decline (*Source*: Census Commissioner, Census India). Therefore, in 2010 more children were vulnerable to abuse than they were five years ago, that is, at the time of publication of the 2005 report. That means, even though the total number of births in the State has decreased the rate of incidence of abuse has gone up.

The rate of neglect also was much higher than it was in 2005. The Kerala Government report of 2005 shows 14.6 per cent neglect whereas according to the 2007 study, girl child neglect alone is 61.64 per cent. Although this figure is higher than the present finding, the difference between the 2005 study and the present study is substantial. According to the present study the rate has gone up by 37.40 per cent, which is significantly high in the present context. The situation is thus alarming because the State is, according to the findings, a less safe place for its children, according to the standards of safety outlined earlier in the study.

The number of children who have become victims of more than one kind of abuse is given separately in different tables. Now we shall expound each kind of abuse as they turned out.

Kicks, punches, blows, pulling by the hair, pushing violently, dropping, slapping on the cheeks, intolerable caning, burning with hot spatula, forcing to carry weights beyond the child's capacity, were grouped under physical abuse. If the child develops anxiety, fear, injury, sickness or dies due to indulgence of the kind described it is counted as the result of physical abuse. The study has not considered controlled caning where it is necessary, by teachers of Upper Primary or high school classes or parents, as physical abuse.

According to the estimate, 44,40,334 children have become victims of physical abuse during the period of study. This is 44.36 per cent of the total number of children in the State according to the statement of population available at the time of preparing this report.

Sexual abuse involves more complexities than physical or emotional abuse. Insertion, exposure, molestation, forcing into sodomy and other unnatural sex acts, early introduction into sexuality through coaxing and bullying, using mobile phone porno to induce a child into sexuality, trapping or inducing into sex acts through internet chat, seducing a child through mobile phone SMS, sodomising the child after intoxicating him, showing porn pictures and other sexually explicit materials, offering money and sweets to sexually trap children, offering employment to traffic children, and failure on the part of the responsible individual to effectively monitor and control excessive sexuality in children were considered sexual abuse. The mental shock the child suffers due to these acts has also been taken as sexual abuse. According to the estimate of the present study, 39.30 per cent children, which means 3,93,38,392 out of the given population of 1,00,09,769 were victims of sexual abuse.

The statistics of abuse released by the Social Welfare Department of Kerala in their 2005 study (the report by the Ministry of Women and Child Development in 2007 stands out) reports rate of sexual abuse which is less than the findings of the present study. This does not imply that some amount of duplication is involved in the process. Because when we consider the fall in the number of children in the State according to the 2011 census, we shall have to believe that the rate of abuse has gone up irrespective of the decrease in child population. It must be remembered in this context that the young people under consideration were those below eighteen years each time. When 18 per cent children out of the total in 2005 (an aggregate of 50 per cent according to MWCD 2007) was reported sexually abused, during the period of this study 39.30 per cent was found in this category. The rise in the percentage of sexual abuse is striking.

Frequent accusations, frequent insults, use of abusive language, terrorizing, threats of sexual abuse, calling the child a nuisance and a burden, humiliating, maligning, gulling, cheating the child with offers, making the child eat leftover food, and confinement were looked at as emotional abuse. Shutting up in a room is solitary confinement. Tying to a tree, or putting on fetters were also taken as emotional abuse although they are physical abuse as well. Denial of medical care, evading, ostracising, giving more work than the child can afford to do, not allowing to sleep well were included under emotional abuse. Since this sort of abuse will shun the growth of the child, no immediate external indicators are necessary. Circumstantial evidence can tell what was happening to the child. According to the data given in Table 1, 59 per cent, or 59,05,764 out of the total suffered emotional abuse during the focal period.

Substance abuse, which in other words is drug abuse, has increased from 6 per cent (2005) to 13.23 per cent (average of boys and girls, present study). According to the present survey,

23.46 per cent male children and 3 per cent female children are either victims or addicts of substances that injure their health. Pan masala, palm wine (toddy), illicit country liquor, Indian made foreign liquor (IMFL), sensual pills, opiates, semi opioids like buprenorphine and even the white liquid substance used as an eraser are consumed to induce pleasure. The children who admitted consumption of opiates were more in the towns and cities than in the villages. [A nexus of drug addict adolescents using brown sugar (heroin) and opioids like buprenorphine has been operating in and around Thiruvalla, a town in Pathanamthitta district.] In the villages they consume pan masala, toddy, country made liquor, and IMFL. The children gainfully employed and those with unchecked financial support freely consumed IMFL. In the cities of Thiruvananthapuram and Kochi this investigator encountered students of High school classes under the impact of sensual pills. Some parents admitted that they do not question their wards even when they are found intoxicated. Consumption of alcohol has almost become a fashion among children in the school final and higher secondary stage.

Physical abuse and emotional abuse have increased when compared to 2005 statistics. The number of children who were physically abused was 24.86 per cent higher than the 2005 report. Sexual abuse was higher by 21.30 per cent than it was in 2005. The increase in emotional abuse was 2.40 per cent more than the 2005 report and 18.30 per cent than the 2007 report. Substance abuse too had gone up by 7.23 per cent from the rate of incidence in 2005. The state of child abuse is therefore, critical in the State.

Victims of Physical, Emotional, Ethical and Social Neglect

Table 1 indicates that child abuse in the context of this study and in the context of contemporary Kerala has increased noticeably. The survey indicates neglect of different kind widespread in the State.

Even while the physical environment is not entirely against growth, giving up care, leaving the child in unsafe circumstances, consciously and deliberately ignoring the child's need for basic necessities like food, shelter, hygiene, safety and health in a manner that would impair the child's growth, such acts of omission were considered serious physical neglect. They are serious because such acts of neglect can either take the child's life, or cause permanent change in character or disposition. Leaving the child to the care of those who were incapable of caring them or were dangerous to them was also taken to be physical neglect. With the former statistics on neglect in the background it is evident that the present study projects a number which is considerably high.

An attitude of unconcern even if the children were one's own, viz., ignoring even if one found his child indulging in unhealthy practices like smoking, drug abuse or alcoholism, or having unhealthy friendship were included under neglect of the emotional kind. Extreme behaviours like demanding actions/work that are well beyond the capacity of the child, and excessive care that retards natural growth are also neglect of this kind. A large percentage of abusive adults fall into this category.

It is commonly agreed that child rearing by adults and child behaviour towards adults have changed radically resulting in circumstances that are not conducive to the well-being children and the society that these children will make later in their life. Parents and care givers/guardians can talk ill of a tradition in which children have been brought up, or ignore or even encourage when children misbehave with people who ought to be respected, or when they are cruel towards their own kind or animals. Adult members of the family including natural parents can create an atmosphere that encourage children to behave insultingly towards their relatives and elders. They can also abstain from educating their children to respect the nation or not encourage the children to pursue studies that might make them useful citizens. This will bar the child from receiving recognition and encouragement and growth through education. Of the 3210 samples, 52 per cent have been found to be under neglect of the kind described.

Earlier studies (2005 and 2007) didn't look upon such aspects of neglect as were examined in the present study. They studied total neglect. The rate of increase in neglect shown here is increase in total neglect. Looking at the problem in this manner, the children who suffered neglect according to this study is 52 per cent or 520 out of every 1000. This is 37.40 per cent higher than the 2005 study. Of the samples surveyed, with the currently available child population in the state 52,05,080 children suffer neglect of this kind.

Intensity of Abuse and the Impact on Children

Data regarding fatal impact of abuse on children have been obtained from media reports and interviews—like death due to physical torture (Ernakulam), throwing one's own child into the canal with an intent to kill (Alappuzha—Kuttanad), suicide due to pedophilic abuse by tourist (Kottayam—Kumarakom), and filial sexual abuse leading to suicide brought to light by CBI (Kaviyoor—Pathanamthitta District). Police crime records have not provided data of this kind. The fate of children who have been kidnapped and trafficked, whether they were dead or alive, was not known. They were simply missing. Some children were trafficked with an offer of employment outside but landed in flesh trade, or as Jockeys on camels in the race. (Cf. poem by famous Malayalam poet P. Bhaskaran "Puthiya kayattumathi"—"The New Export"). But there was no proper record on it barring media reports, and a few court cases. It was therefore legitimate to consider that the children went missing had done so as a result of abuse or neglect, and at the moment they are either victims of abuse or are the ones who suffer the aftermath of abuse, or in extreme cases, are dead. The official list of State Crime Records Bureau of children reported missing is given in Table 4.

The statistics in Table 4, which shows the official number of children reported missing during the span of this study is only the tip of an ice berg. The highest incidence of missing according to the SCRB was in the capital city of Thiruvananthapuram, followed by Kollam district. Malappuram which is dominated by the Muslim community from where, witnesses have testified, both male and female children have left for gulf countries with or without parental permission. Not all issues of missing children might have been reported to the police. The official figure of missing children therefore does not in any case project the actual volume of disappearance. Out of a hundred and thirty samples taken from Malappuram district, 17 children reported knowledge of children below eighteen leaving for gulf countries in search of employment.

TABLE 4

Details of Children reported missing during 2010

District	No. of Missing Children		
	Male	Female	Total
Thiruvananthapuram	81	129	210
Kollam	58	86	144
Pathanamthitta	10	28	38
Alappuzha	24	29	53
Kottayam	12	18	30
Idukki	26	31	57
Ernakulam	28	36	64
Thrissur	22	42	64
Palakkad	10	15	25
Malappuram	44	27	71
Kozhikode	28	25	53
Wynad	12	7	19
Kannur	16	11	27
Kasaragod	16	6	22
Total	387	490	877

Source: IG of Police, State Crime Records Bureau, Thiruvananthapuram.

Apart from children lost due to neglect and indifference on the part of the parents and care-givers, the rate of kidnap for despicable ends was rampant in the state. The official statement (SCRB) of kidnap for the year 2010 (till November) furnished that 102 children, male and female, were kidnapped, with 24 from Thiruvananthapuram district and 27 from Kollam district. The latter is the highest in the state.

Physical abuse and emotional (psychological) abuse have left children to suffer the rest of their lives. Children who have fallen victim to drugs and alcohol, have not been able to pursue learning for self-development. Some have lasting injuries of burns, or carry the weight of failure to thrive. The victims of sexual abuse betray traits of imbalance and have a tendency to become abusers. According to the survey, among young adults 56 out of 1000 were victims of severity of abuse.

Most of the abused children were victims of abuse which might not leave any permanent impairment, but which will give them sufficient trouble during their early years of growth. 714 out of 1000 child samples observed were victims of temporary shocks, swellings on body, fear due to threats by elders at home and bullies at school, and mild anxiety.

It was found that the intensity of total abuse was on the increase. The types of abuse were recorded and the magnitude of abuse ascertained from the manner in which the abuse was reported. This was done after direct interaction with the children and young adults and interviews with parents and other stakeholders. A comparison with the earlier reports on abuse in this region has helped to determine the level of increase in the fatality of physical abuse, and also increase in sexual abuse and cases of child disappearance. Of each 1000 samples, 183 were found to have been victims of abuse that was agonizing to them.

The report of 2007 indicates increased rate of agonising abuse in comparison with the 2005 report. According to the estimate of this study the rate has gone higher again. The Table 5 indicates estimate of abuse of all kind. The victims identified belong to all walks of life—apart from victims belonging to seemingly well off or working class families, they include children of habitual drunkards, drug addicts, adulterers, and male and female sex workers.

TABLE 5

Type of abuse	Estimate according to present findings		Estimate according to earlier findings	
	Total child victims	Victims per 1000	2005 per 1000	2007 per 1000
Physical abuse	44,40,334	444	195	561
Sexual abuse	39,33,839	393	180	500
Emotional abuse	59,05,764	590	566	407
Substance abuse	26,48,585*	265*	60	—
Neglect	52,05,080	520	146	616 (Girl child neglect) (total population: 49,19,369)

Source: The table gives the number of child victims of one or more types of ill-treatment.

* Total of male and female.

Victims of Agnonising Abuse

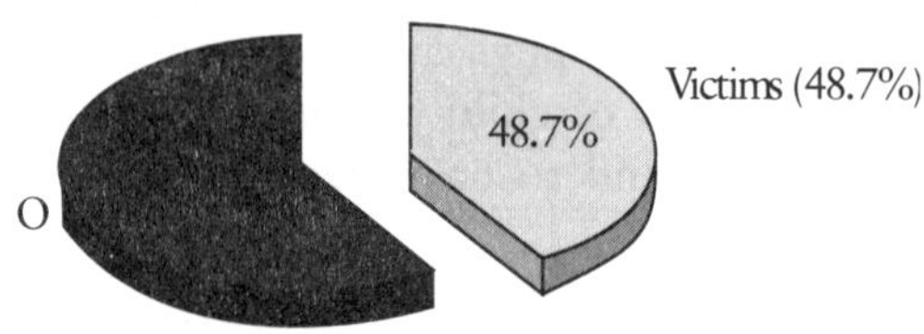

That means 487 in every 1000 are victims of agonizing abuse (this does not include substance abuse). In other words one child out of every three in the literate society of Kerala suffers at least one type of agonizing abuse.

Gender, Age, and Abuse

6

Gender and Abuse

In the national context it is estimated that female children are more abused than the male children. In the case of Kerala however, boys are more vulnerable to abuse than girls. Table 1 shows rate of abuse according to gender. Rate of abuse varies according to gender.

TABLE 1

Gender difference and Rate of Abuse

Abuse type	Population of male children: 50,90,400 Boys out of 1000	Population of female children: 49,19,369 Girls out of 1000
Physical abuse	467	424
Sexual abuse	406	382
Emotional abuse	575	605
Substance abuse	235	30
Neglect	470	560

When maltreatment of all types were considered, male children were found more at risk in the State. They were more physically abused than girls for many reasons. This was because more boys than girls were thrashed at home, more boys than girls venture outside home at odd hours, more boys than girls go to work, and at school they are more bullied than girls.

Gender-wise Physical Abuse

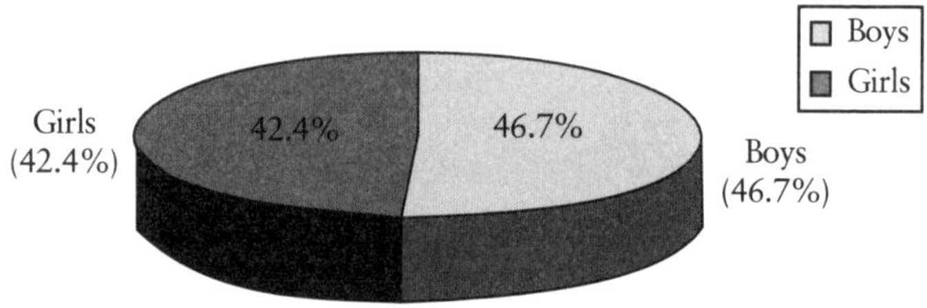

More boys become victims of sexual abuse than girls. When 406 boys out of 1000 were victims of sexual abuse, 382 girls out of 1000 were victims of the same. The difference was, therefore, significant. The high rate of incidence of sexual abuse of boys was reported from the northern districts of Kerala, with Malappuram topping.

Gender-wise Sexual Abuse

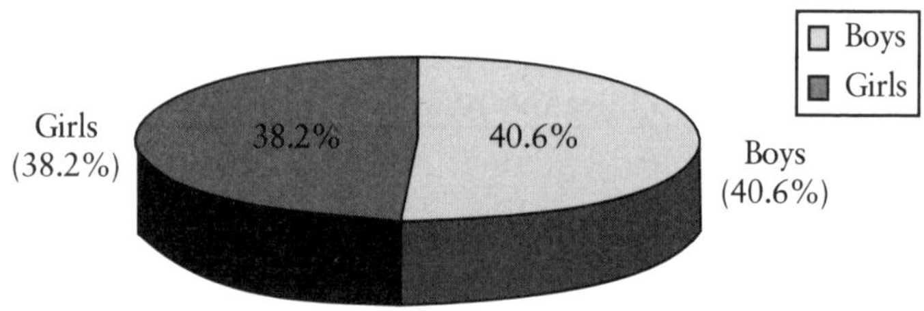

Historically, even in matrilineal communities, the marginal status and therefore the vulnerability, was characteristic of the female gender. Recent changes in the social set up and attitude to life have contributed to the increase of sexual abuse of girls including rape and murder. Numerous reports in the print and electronic media sufficiently strengthen the present findings. The statement of child rape for the period of study issued by the State Crime Records Bureau is presented in the following Table 2.

TABLE 2

Number of rape cases reported under crimes against children act (Jan. to Dec. 2010)

District	Number of children raped
Thiruvananthapuram	42
Kollam	32
Pathanamthitta	10
Alappuzha	6
Kottayam	17
Idukki	9
Ernakulam	21
Thrissur	12
Palakkad	12
Malappuram	7
Kozhikode	16
Wynad	8
Kannur	6
Kasaragod	8
Total	206

Table 2 shows the rape cases registered under Crimes Against Children Act. 206 incidents of child rapes were registered till November in the year 2010. The highest incidence of child rape was reported from the two southern districts of the State, Thiruvananthapuram and Kollam. The "official" record, and as usual, only the tip of an ice berg.

Child Rape in 2010 (Police Record)

Official statement of child rape pertains to abuse of female children. 'Rape' of boys too happen—the investigator has been informed of the 'rape' threats of boys of the age group 14-17 hailing from Malappuram district. Such threats have horrified the boys who were threatened, who fearing 'rape' did not go to school to take their examinations. These attempts are however seldom recorded.

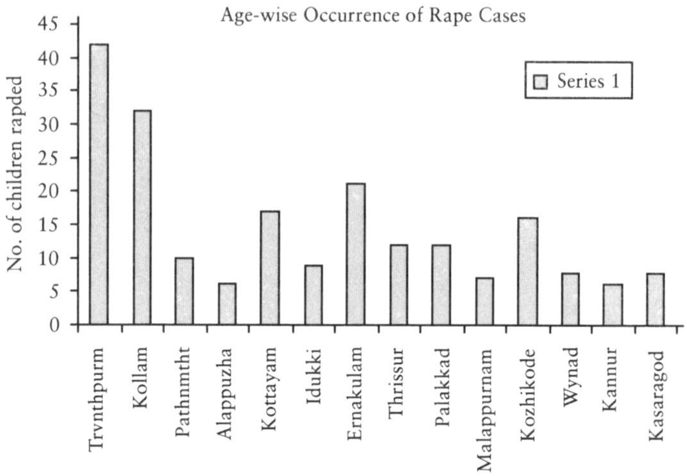

Emotional abuse: Emotional abuse has increased considerably in the case of both genders. In the 2005 report, 540 boys and 570 girls out of 1000 are shown to have suffered emotional abuse; during the period of this study it increased to 575 out of 1000 for boys and 605 out of 1000 for girls. For emotional abuse, the difference noted in this study was narrow between the two genders.

Emotional Abuse 2005

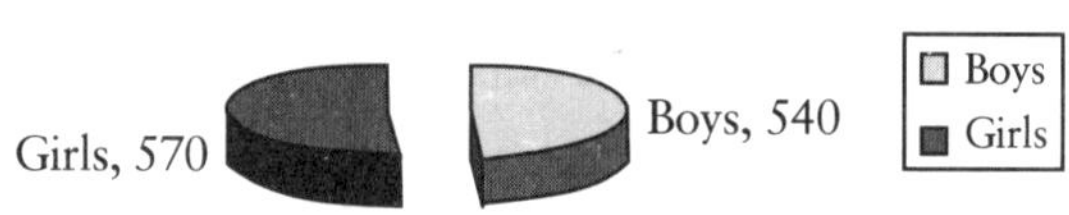

Emotional Abuse 2010

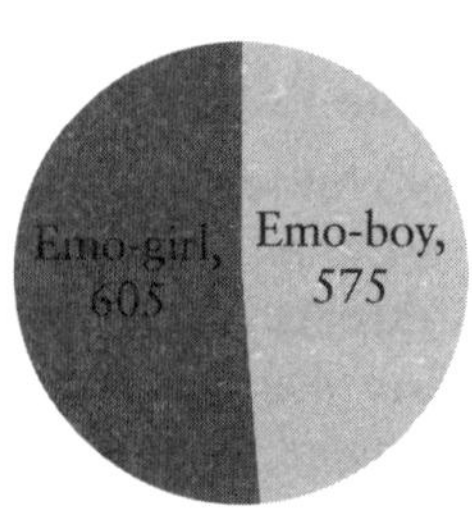

Substance abuse is high in boys and low in girls. Most instances of substance abuse in female children were found in the district of Kollam in the south of Kerala. In all the districts of Kerala substance abuse is on the increase among boys. While 235 boys out of 1000 admitted abuse of this kind, only 30 girls did that. That means, of the substance abusive children the brute majority are boys (89 per cent). The researcher has witnessed more girls talking about liquor in the presence of boys and perhaps by wanting to induce this behaviour in the boys they covertly express their own desire for alcohol the consumption of which by females is still a taboo in the State.

Gender-wise Substance Abuse

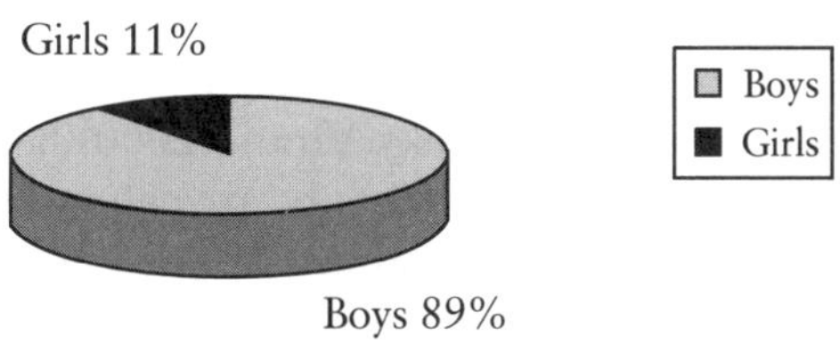

Neglect: The occurrence of physical, emotional and ethical neglect together considered do not show much difference between male and female children when compared with the earlier study. 470 boys and 560 girls in 1000 were under neglect. There was a little hike in the case of boys as more boys come under difficulties due to physical neglect. This was supported by what was seen in direct observation.

Gender-wise Neglect

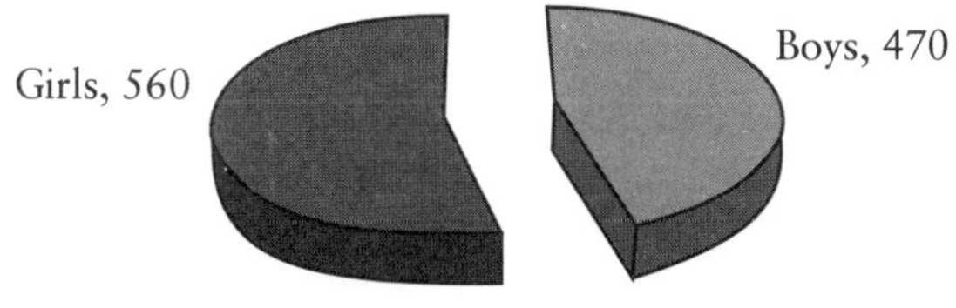

Age and Abuse

Age of the children brought under this study was between 10 and 18. That this attempt could not take up the rest was a limitation. However, the core, or the most abused children, come under this age group. Although Pinky Virani's *Bitter Chocolate* postulates that child abuse begins at an earlier stage, due to limitations the present process could not undertake an exhaustive investigation of abuse of child of every age. Although extreme situations of physical abuse of infants like Manchausean's Syndrome by Proxy do exist, this abuse is widely manifest after the early years. As the child is not emotionally developed during infanthood, emotional abuse also is not possible.

During infanthood mothers under Manchausean's syndrome by proxy (See annexure II) physically abuse their babies to make them sick; psychopaths physically or sexually abuse infants to gratify their urge. Pinky Virani (2000) has cited a few instances of sexual abuse of infants by psychopaths. Although this can happen in all cultures, abuse of this kind is not found in large numbers in comparison with what happens to children of a higher age group. As direct data collection from lower age group is outside the scope of this work, the researcher has relied on other sources for such information.

Adolescent respondents reported that sexual abuse happens mostly between 12 and 17. Responses collected from children below 18 also show that this is the most vulnerable period. The present study found rate of sex abuse increasing according to age among children between the age group of 10-17. The same is the case of emotional abuse. The following chart shows percentage of sexual abuse according to age.

Age-wise Occurrence of Sexual Abuse

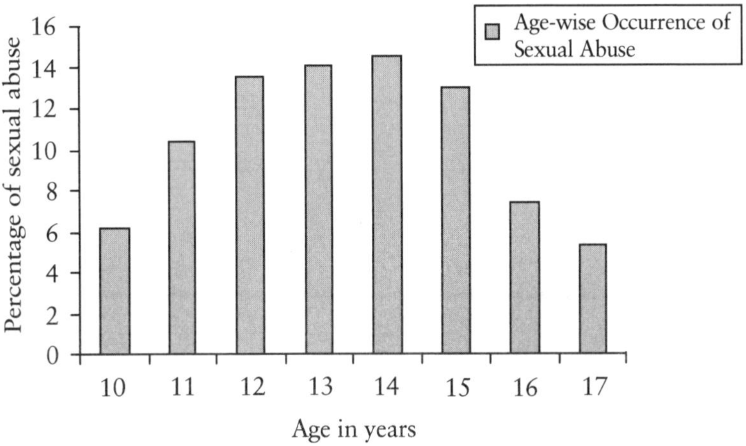

Both sexual and emotional abuse were found to increase steadily with age, between 10 and 18. Maximum sexual and emotional abuse cases were found to be occurring during the period from 12th to 15th year (percentage of occurrence from the tenth year shown vertically). 84.8 per cent of sexual abuse was found to take place from the age of 10 to 17 and 83.3 per cent of emotional abuse was found to happen during the same period.

Occurrence of Sexual and Emotional Abuse, 10-17 Years

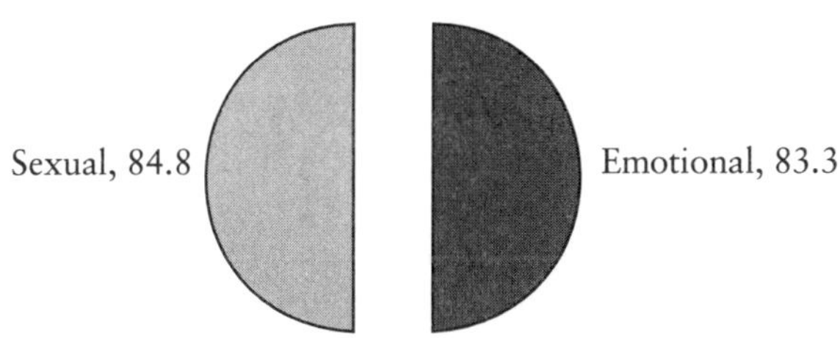

Neglect also increases as the child advances in age. Between the age of 10 and 12 the rate is 282 out of 1000. Between 13 and 17 it is 587 out of 1000. This indicates that the children in this age group are more victims of emotional abuse. The physical and psychological circumstances of the parents and care-givers influence and determine the nature of the neglect.

Neglect between Ten and Seventeen

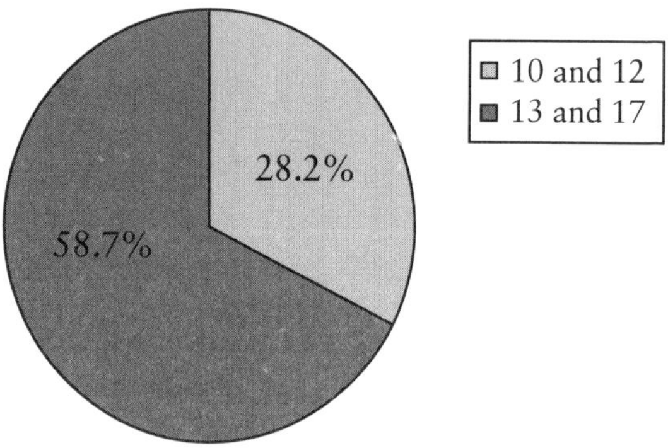

Age-wise Percentage of Neglect

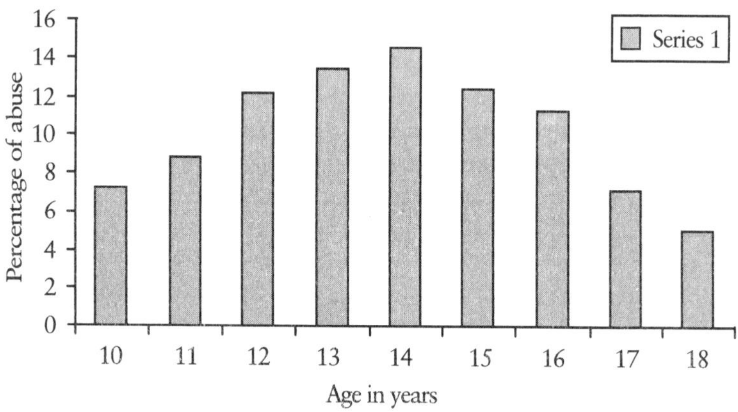

The foregoing analysis gives that maltreatment is the highest in children between 10 and 17. The data proves that more boys are maltreated than girls. And contrary to belief, it was found that more boys become victims of sexual abuse than girls. However, according to the findings more girls are emotionally abused and more girls are neglected than boys. In all the districts of Kerala substance abuse was found to be on the increase among boys.

7

Family Environment in Kerala and Child Abuse

Factors that affect environment in the family set up are—education of the parents, their income, social status, their acceptance or respectability in their own community, whether the family is nuclear or joint, the presence or absence of parents at home, whether the lifestyle is rural or urban; and their attitude to life evidenced by discipline or indiscipline. In the case of abuse at home, the nature of the parent's job is a factor. Those who are without employment idling away their time can cause more harm to the children than one who is employed away in the Gulf region. The unemployed parent, due to frustration, can assault their children physically and verbally causing serious physical and/or psychological damage. Parents who are employed in the Gulf countries and other far away places leave the children with their own parents where they either enjoy unchecked freedom or are under strict surveillance both of which are harmful to growth and therefore abusive. The children who are left in the hostels are vulnerable to substance abuse, and sexual abuse.

In this chapter the influence of two major factors on child abuse, namely presence/absence of parents at home and indiscipline evidenced by alcoholism are examined.

With an unemployed parent staying at home the rate of total maltreatment was found to be high. Total maltreatment was more in the cases of children whose both parents were employed in distant places. However, their absence could not have been reason to emotional neglect. In most instances the caretakers of children whose parents were away were their own grandparents or close relatives. When the parents living with the children were away at work during day time, the children

TABLE 1

Presence/absence of Parents at Home and Percentage of Abuse

Type of abuse	Parent unemployed (present at home)	Parent employed (present)	Parent employed (absent)
Total maltreatment	56.4	40.3	57.5
Physical abuse	66.4	42.3	57.5
Sexual abuse	19.3	32.4	44.2
Emotional abuse	69.6	38.1	54.7
Neglect	70.1	48.2	73.4

in more than 90% cases were at school or they were supposed to be so. From direct interviews with children and teachers it was found that not all children really reach school. Instances of boys and girls got entangled in sexual and substance abuse were reported. In the villages, where the unemployed father remained at home, the rate of physical and emotional abuse was high.

Abuse Rate Among Children with Alcoholic Parents

Abu Zaid Harsan who travelled Kerala in the tenth century observed that the people of Kerala never did anything immoral or improper and that everyone seemed to dislike intoxicating drinks (K.N. Ezhuthachan, 1992:17). Ibn Khurdad, a ninth century visitor to Kerala, had more or less the same opinion about the people of Kerala. Barbarosa recorded in 1515 that the Nairs of Kerala would not drink toddy (palm wine—an alcoholic drink) even if threatened with death. Drinking became common only after the eighteenth century (Elamkulam 1970).

The 'deconstruction' of Kerala culture, an adjunct of the British rule, was in favour of religious conversion and alcoholism. In the first decade of the twenty-first century alcohol consumption in the State showed steady increase. Abuse rate among children with alcoholic parents was found to be higher than those who have non-alcoholic parents. Alcohol is a booster device for all types of abuse.

The official statement of the sale of alcoholic drinks through the retail outlets of Kerala State Beverages Corporation alone is astonishing. Table 2 gives the sale of Indian made foreign liquor by KSBC retail outlets during the period April 2007 to December 2010.

TABLE 2

Consumption of Alcohol in Kerala

Year	Consumption of alcohol in bulk litres		Money spent in crores of rupees
	IMFL	Beer	
April 2007 to March 2008	13,27,91,938	4,56,94,736	3,669.41
April 2008 to March 2009	15,36,17,992	5,50,72,756	4,630.95
April 2009 to March 2010	16,86,85,871	6,64,89,949.48	5,539.84
April 2010 to December 2010	14,42,58,915	4,48,16,302	4,912.80

Source: Kerala State Beverages Corporation Ltd., Thiruvananthapuram.

The average monthly sales of Indian made foreign liquor (IMFL) from April 2007 to March 2008 through KSBC alone was 1,10,65,995 bulk litres. 38,07,895 litres of beer also was sold. The money spent by the buyers in this way was rupees 305.78 crores. That means, during this period, everyday, Keralites spent rupees 10.19 crores to intoxicate themselves with alcohol bought from the government outlets. From April to December in 2010 Keralites bought 14,42,58,915 litres of IMFL and 4,48,16,302 litres of beer spending rupees 4912.80 crores. This implies in the year 2010, each day during the specified period, Keralites consumed 5,34,292.28 litres of IMFL and 1,65,986.30 litres of beer, spending 18.20 crores of rupees. There is great increase in the consumption of alcohol by Keralites in just three years—the money spent on liquor had almost doubled. The amount spent on it if constructively employed in creating employment for the unemployed, can, apart from nourishing the society of Kerala in other ways, reduce the present rate of child maltreatment.

It has been assessed by several newspapers that the amount spent on alcohol by the drunkards of the state is higher than the total spending on rice (the staple food grain of the state) consumption. The amount spent on illicit liquor is not known. With the increased rate of liquor consumption the social situation of Kerala at the moment could be conceived as one that is precariously balanced. Alcohol induced abuse during the study period is discernible in the following Table 3 which shows abuse in alcohol consuming and non-alcohol consuming families.

TABLE 3

Child Abuse in Alcohol Consuming and Non-alcohol Consuming Families

Type of abuse	Families with alcoholic parent/adult (number of children reporting abuse—out of 1000)	Families without alcoholic parent/adult (number of children reporting abuse—out of 1000)	Difference
Physical abuse	334	86	248
Sexual abuse	308	76	232
Emotional abuse	394	186	208
Substance abuse	199	26	173
Neglect	319	211	108

The difference between families with an alcoholic parent and without was significant. The children in families without alcoholic adults were found to be safer than those with them. However, it was probable that the child who reported had mixed up abuse by non-alcoholics in the family/outside as well. This is a limitation indeed.

The survey indicated that children in the families with alcoholic parents were more under one or other or more than one abuse than the children in families without alcoholics. In non-alcoholic families the rate of abuse was considerably low. Therefore, in the present context in Kerala children are at more risk because the number of drinking adults has been going up at an exponential rate. Dr. V. Sathish, Head of the Department of Psychiatry, Kottayam Government Medical College, observed that when alcohol is in control of the nervous system the alcoholic who becomes aggressive also develops mental disorders. That part of the human brain that discriminates right and wrong, ill functions resulting in the surfing of baser aspects of behaviour like anger, hatred, suspicion, enmity, revenge and concern about one's own incompatibilities. When all this surge at the same moment the individual becomes evil. Thus the alcoholic becomes a perpetrator of abuse even if at the core of his heart he dislikes to be one.

During the study it was recorded that physical abuse was the highest in alcoholic families. Hair pulling, throwing away, slapping on the face, kicks and blows were reported by the victims of abusive parents. Some attacks by drunken males are violent to the extent of being fatal. 334 children out of 1000 have reported abuse of this kind. Among the children of non-alcoholic parents physical abuse of this kind was very less. Only 86 out of 1000 have reported physical abuse of this magnitude. (In the middle of May 2012, in an incident of drunken violence in Manarcaud, Kottayam District, a seven-year-old girl was lacerated with a knife head to foot by her father. Only the local Police could rescue the child by taking her to Kottayam Medical College. The drunken abuser, Kochumon, a granite quarry worker, later committed suicide by hanging.)

The risk of sexual abuse is high in alcoholic families. The difference is spectacular, 308 against 76.

Emotional abuse was the highest in families with alcoholic adults. It was reported that the vocabulary after drinking was mostly profane and detrimental to the child's self-esteem. Some respondents disclosed that it was sometimes intolerable. 394 out of 1000 children in alcoholic families were emotionally abused whereas in families without an alcoholic member the abuse rate was almost half.

In the present socio-cultural context it isn't a rare phenomenon that both the parents are alcoholics. Yet not many women in Kerala willfully break the canon that women should abstain from consuming alcoholic drinks. Hence, still not many women in Kerala, especially in the villages, consume alcohol. Many men who are very spiritual or too traditional or too disciplined do not consume intoxicants like alcohol. However, it is a proven fact that alcoholism is on the increase and it has spoiled the lives of many children because not only adults at home but teachers too come forward in large numbers to drink alcohol. Alcohol consumption by a teacher was considered unethical till a generation ago, but now it has become commonplace.

This according to the adult respondents, signal a sorry state. Substance abuse, especially alcoholism in children, is naturally high in alcohol consuming families.

Children of drunkards experience more neglect than the children of non-drinking parents or guardians. Different neglects have been defined earlier. Children of non-drinking parents experience lesser physical and/or emotional neglect than those who are otherwise. Habitual consumers of alcohol have this or other mental faculty in some unhealthy state with the result that they are hardly able to pay respect to ethical aspects of living. Consequently, ethical neglect will be high among alcoholic parents and caretakers. In this study it is found that ethical neglect is two-fold in this case. The State of affairs of the children of alcoholics who are not employed is worse.

In the State of Kerala alcoholism and child abuse seem to work in unison. The sheer number of children abused by drinking adults is a clear indicator. Drug addiction too is there just behind alcoholism. The enormity of sale of Indian made foreign liquor through government owned retail outlets and the money people spend on it indicate the unsavory atmosphere prevailing at most households. This atmosphere is not congenial to the balanced growth of children who are the nation's future.

The assumption with which this section on alcoholism and abuse began was that alcohol is a booster device of all types of abuse. The findings so far support this assumption. The investigator had put questions to the children about parental behaviour and alcoholism. To the questions on the causes of child abuse the adult respondents invariably proposed alcoholism as one. In descending order, alcoholic adults topped abuse in emotional, physical, and sexual types. Among alcoholic abusers there were family members and others who were familiar to the child or the child's family.

Of the total emotionally abused children in the family set up, 39.4 per cent had drunken abusers. This shows that the risk of emotional abuse is highest in addicts, whether of alcohol or drugs. In the case of physically abused children 33.4 per cent were abused by alcoholics. Sex abuse in majority of cases met was initiated by perpetrators who were not the natural parents of the child. Among the sexually abusive perpetrators in the family setup the majority were addicts.

Abuse Rate of Children in Alcohol Consuming and Non-alcohol Consuming Families

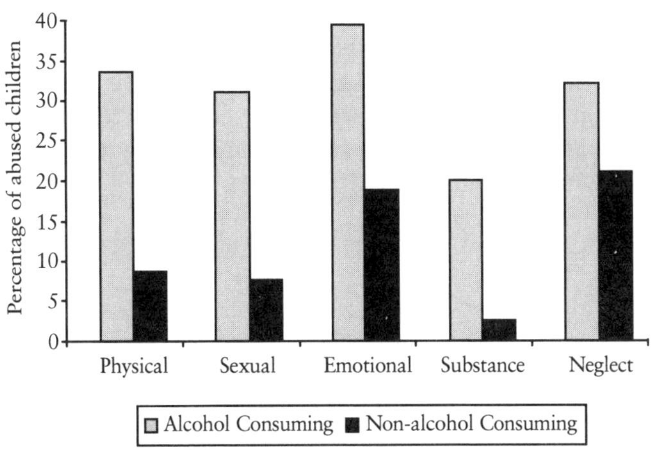

Questionnaires to the adults reveal that alcoholism among the adult male members of the family might lead to the younger boys in the family taking to alcohol at an early age and thus abuse happens through transfer or influence of an unhealthy adult practice (R.K. Sreekumaran Chettiar, Joint Commissioner,

Kerala Excise, accepts that the volume of consumption of alcohol has been increasing every year and that a considerable number of consumers of Indian made foreign liquor are adolescent males, although law forbids sale of liquor to those below the age of 21). Alcoholism, as mentioned earlier is fast becoming common in the State. At the moment in the state one out of every three children suffers drug and alcohol caused abuse. The harshness of the impact of abuse is many fold if the parents are addicts of both drug and alcohol.

On 13-6-09 Former DGP Alexander in DD Malayalam TV Channel said: "It is surprising how the youngsters in the schools and colleges—despite the overwhelming presence of college unions—get into the hands of the underworld men. Of the underworld denizens many are drug dealers. What is this nexus? Are the police involved? Are the rich business people involved?" When a DGP cannot single out the reason why the presence of students in crime gangs is increasing, perhaps the psychologist and the social worker can. Sufficient evidence indicate swell in the habit of alcoholism. Conflict within the family is already on the increase due to a variety of factors, resulting in added consumption of alcohol. Naturally the number of drunken, irresponsible and abusive fathers are increasing. Unpleasant homes drive children towards easy money making and pleasure hunt. Consequently they become prey to human 'predators'.

Child Abuse and Socio-economic Factors

8

The Economic Status of the Family and Child Abuse

During investigation the income of the child's family and the education of the parents were recorded. The income disclosed was the one recorded in the family's ration card, which was usually below the actual figure. However, from the disclosures on education and employment of the parent(s) the investigator could estimate the financial status of the family. Moreover, the question whether BPL (Below Poverty Line) or APL (Above Poverty Line) brought an answer to the economic status of parents which is surely one of the causes of the problem.

The economically weak can at certain point shed their backwardness with money coming from some quarter. However, at the moment of collection of data those who were in the BPL category were treated as economically backward.

It isn't that only the economically low turn out to be abusive. In fact abuse of the sexual kind is not less in the higher income groups. If the parents have an education below tenth standard and have a BPL status the economic status will be low. Consequently, the parents may not claim a high status in the contemporary social set up. The argument is that physical and emotional abuse and neglect are also congenital to the socio-economic status of the parents.

Children from BPL families are more prone to physical abuse than those from APL families. In the context of Kerala and in fact in the context of human society in general, there are parents who are well intentioned but who owing to financial stringencies and pressures indulge in physical abuse of their children. Since children are mostly unaware of the pressures of the parents, report their excited or angry behaviour as abuse. There were no means to filter out such reports. However all reports and indicators

TABLE 1

Economic status of the family and child abuse
Percentage of children reporting abuse

Type of abuse	Economic status	
	BPL (% of abuse)	APL (% of abuse)
Physical abuse	63	49
Sexual abuse	34.20	33
Emotional abuse	69	56
Substance abuse	25	21
Neglect	57	52

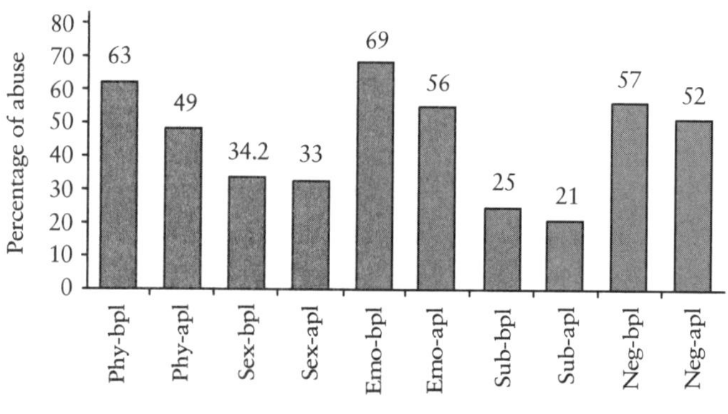

Percentage of children reporting abuse in BPL and APL families

suggest that in comparison with APL families, struggle for day-to-day existence might lead to harsh behaviour leading to physical abuse by the parents belonging to the category BPL.

Physical Abuse According to Economic Status

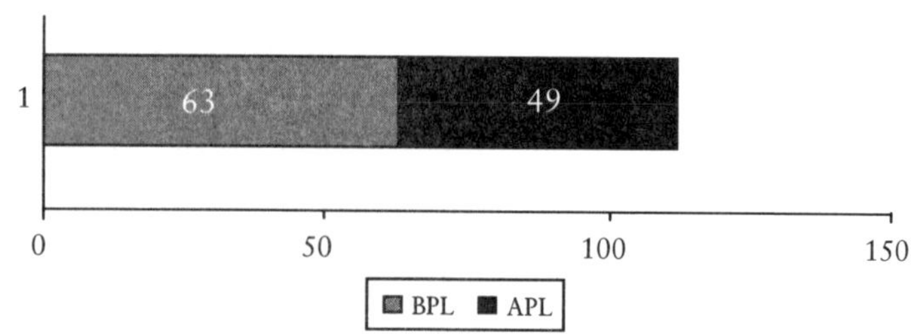

Lack of sufficient exposure to the ways of the world, and lack of awareness about the impact of abuse on the child's growth have added intensity to abuse of children in those BPL families that have been reported abusive. Since the entire population of the State is victim to the pressures of the neo-liberal tendencies of the market, struggle for possessing commodities that make life seem comfortable is tragically high in low income group families. This was evidenced in the response of a set of low income group children belonging to Panakachira village in the east of Kottayam district. The children invited to an interactive session organized by this investigator appeared to be enthusiastic and clever. During the sessions they showed themselves to be good students. Most of the children were between 10 and 12. Although they were the children of casual workers they expressed desire for owning cars and well equipped houses. The majority of them who were ambitious and anxious about their future were physically and emotionally abused at home. These children seemed not able to comprehend the behaviour of the adults at home. They expressed a mood of despair and even of suicide when they were asked to write about what in their lives touched them most and what disturbed them most. Proper education leading to proper awareness absent, the limitations of the individual, and the infatuation for luxury goods and intoxicating substances which is the child of neo-liberalism have escalated the lay individual's tendency to abuse. This invariably has led to unhappy and sometimes chaotic situations in many such families.

Social and economic backwardness together with the tendency to escape into the temporary pleasures that drug or alcohol offers have caused lack of regard for values and loss of restraint in adults. Here the children who are the victims of such adults who include their own parents become objects of uncontrollable anger, receive serious injuries on mind and body.

Low income and the consequent inability to grow through education—recall Kerala Model which roughly means achieving economic growth through education—and attaining a decent social status is still a barrier to a sizable portion of the population, and, although the present endeavour cannot go by the long-standing issues related to caste and tribe, it is certain that the human segment classified as socially and economically weak too, along with others, fall under the BPL category.

Going ahead with the social aspects of child abuse, the results of the study indicate that economic and social aspects such as mentioned above are factors that subvert human faculties. This subversion of faculties has been happening to the general populace, let alone the financially weak. Considering the issue from the angle of values, Dr. David, one of the respondents, maintained that as a result of Globalization, there is a strong thought among some people that things that were once considered bad or evil could now be viewed as good. The result is the exponential increase in the rate of sexual abuse. Those who are tenderly associated with the child's psyche like maternal and paternal uncles, grandparents and other close relatives have emerged as sexually abusive. When they sexually abuse the child, s/he undergoes intense mental pressure and develops psychic disorders. Although this cannot be the case with every family, this happens in homes normally conceived safe.

The children from economically and socially weak families, fall easy prey to racketeers, and tourist sex abuse. The present inquiry has revealed that those children with a low socio-economic background are more vulnerable to abuse by racketeers. According to the estimates 342 children out of one thousand reported sexual abuse. The difference between BPL and APL was not significant.

Sexual Abuse According to Economic Status

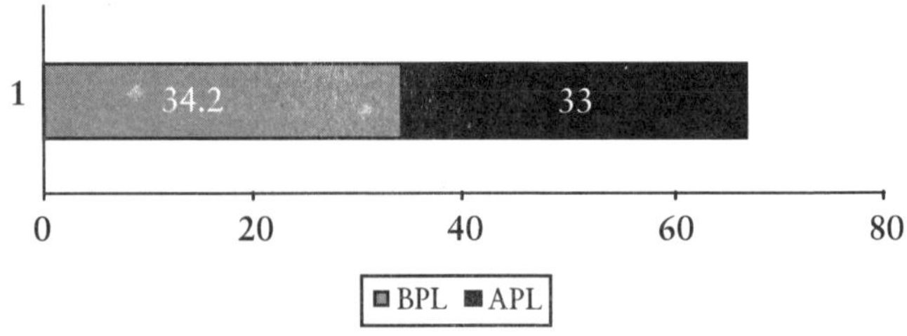

Emotional abuse was higher, almost the double of sexual abuse in any family set-up. In BPL families it was 13 per cent more than that of APL families.

Emotional Abuse According to Economic Status

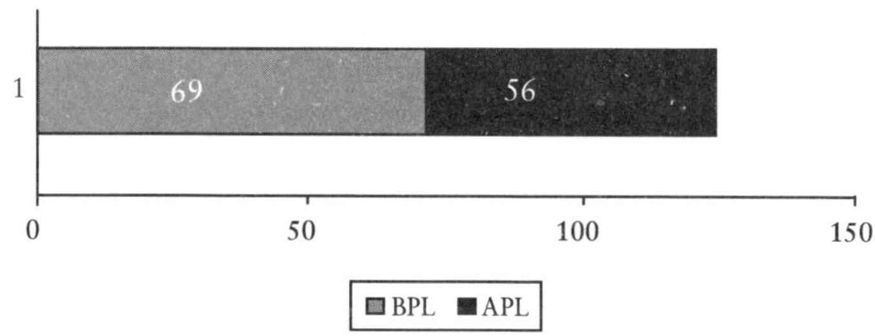

In the samples examined, in BPL families substance abuse was 4 per cent higher than the same in APL families. Abusive substances commonly consumed by the semiliterate and a section of the literate among BPL include toddy ganja which is cultivated in the forest regions, illicit liquor and cheap IMFL. Some children make use of even the white fluid used to erase writing as an intoxicant. In APL families, children and adolescents gratify themselves with opiates and opioids mentioned elsewhere in this study.

Substance Abuse According to Economic Status

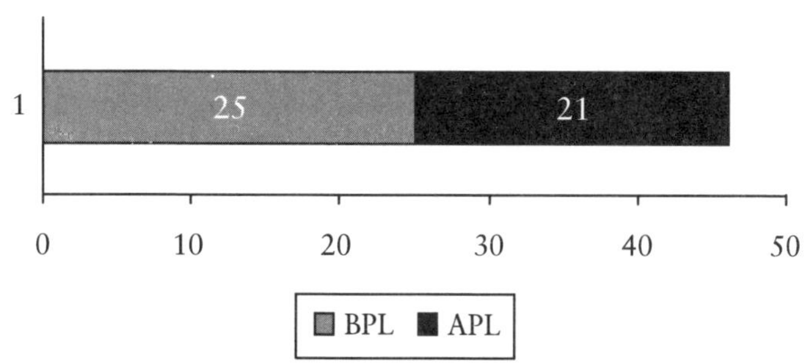

Neglect in BPL families is also higher than that in APL families. Physical, emotional and ethical neglect taken together, was higher by 5 per cent in low income families. Traditionally, the parents of Kerala have wanted their wards to behave well with others and have good education even while they ignored other subtler aspects of child rearing. However, from the data examined so far, it could be assessed that this attitude was on the decline. Ethical neglect was found to be 265 out of 1000 in BPL families and 195 in APL ones.

Neglect According to Economic Status

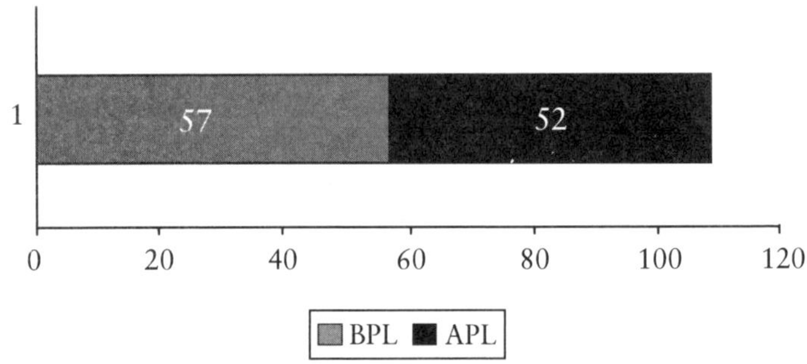

One point worth mention is that in the State of Kerala and also at the national level, abuse and neglect can vary according to the caste/tribe/community to which the child belongs. The treatment the urban child gets at home is not the same as the child belonging to a tribal household gets. Such an attempt based on distinction is not within the purview of this attempt.

Abuse resulting out of both social and economic inferiority was found to be more intense than abuse due to economic backwardness alone. Physical, sexual, emotional and substance abuse and neglect of various kind were rampant in those families that were socially and economically low. In the present social set up of Kerala, those who are not educated, and those who do not think of a way out of the State of depravity are considered socially low even if they have access to income. Such depravity of parents and adults manifests as abuse when a father commits incest and takes his daughter to flesh trade/or they commit suicide (Kothamangalam—Ernakulam district—flesh traffic case involving a father and his daughter, which is at the moment in the court, and the Kaviyoor—Pathanamthitta District—racket caused death case where the father was found to have committed sexual abuse) or when the mother takes her daughter to flesh trade (Alappuzha issue) or the mother's sister acting as the middle person in a sex racket operated by a woman (Kiliroor—Kottayam district—flesh trade in which the victim died). Lure of comfort and luxury accompanied by premature exposure to sexuality through the electronic media and neglect on the part of parents or caretakers prepare ground for an easy glide into the hands of racketeers. However, when the parent himself/herself is the culprit, the error non-pareil occurs.

Family Structure and Abuse

While investigating child abuse it is important to understand with who the child lives at the moment. Those living with legally wedded parents, with paternal or maternal grand-parents, with maternal uncles or aunts, parental uncles or aunts, live in the family set-up. However, present day family set-up has mostly father and mother or either of the two. And some lucky ones may have grandparents living with them. With the institution of marriage becoming fragile, increasing number of married women go back to their parents. And when they go they carry their children too. A section of parents are adoptive parents. Such parents, however, are very few in number. When the child's father or mother remarries there will be a step parent. The children also live with their grandparents when their own parents are away or are not alive. Looking at the problem of children from this angle, the children of Kerala face diverse physical and psychological environment due to the structure the family with which they live. Taking into account each of these factors might be too ambitious for a work such as this. However, during data collection it was possible to identify children living with their own parents, living with single parent and those without parents. Rate of abuse in each of this category was found to be different.

Distribution of Abuse according to Family Structure

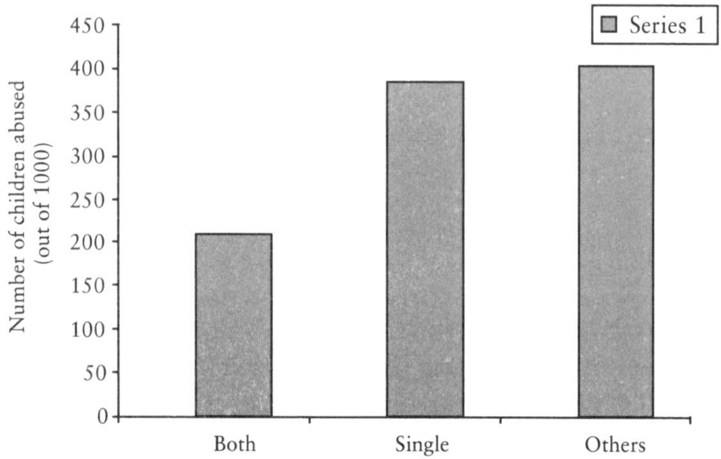

Both: Among children living with both the parents
Single: Among children living with single parent
Others: Among children living with others

Distribution of Abuse According to Family Structure

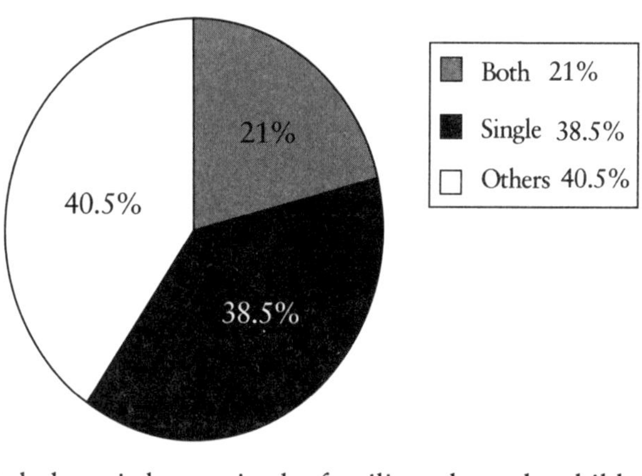

Total abuse is lowest in the families where the children live with their own biological parents. According to the estimates of this study, 21 per cent of the abused children live with both parents. It is much lower than children living with other relatives. When the child lives with single parent, abuse rate is much higher. 38.5 per cent living with single parent suffer abuse. The children living under the care of others are the most abused. Out of the total 40.5 per cent children undergo one or other form of abuse or multiple abuse.

Children who live with their own parents—father and mother—have to suffer less physical abuse than those do not live with their own parents. The estimate according to the input received from children, 21.2 per cent of the total physically abused children live with both parents. In the case of children living with one parent the high risk rate is indicated by the relatively high number of abused children, 36.18 per cent. The case of those who are under the care of others is riskier 42.62 per cent.

Physical Abuse: Distribution According to Family Structure

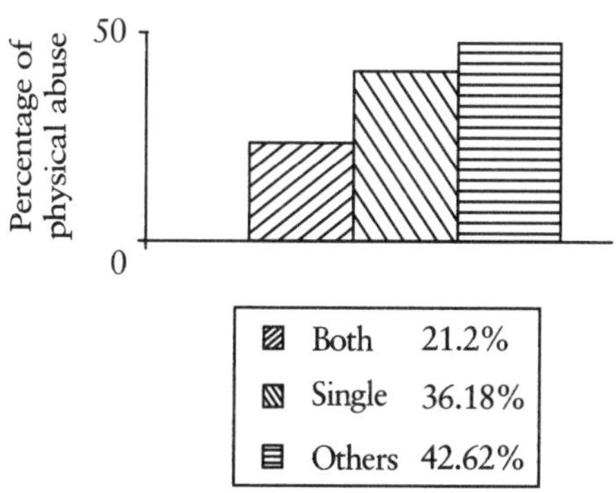

Both: Among children living with their own parents

Single: Among children with single parent

Others: Among children living with caretakers or others

Sexually abused children in the family set up live mostly with single parent or others. The perpetrator of sexual abuse in the majority of the samples was a person known to the child or a close relative. Sexual abuse also was low in families with the biological parents and or grandparents living with the children. According to the estimates of the present study 22 per cent children out of the total sexually abused live with both parents. It is 31 per cent in families with single parent; 47 per cent in the case of children living with others.

Sexual Abuse-Distribution According to Family Structure

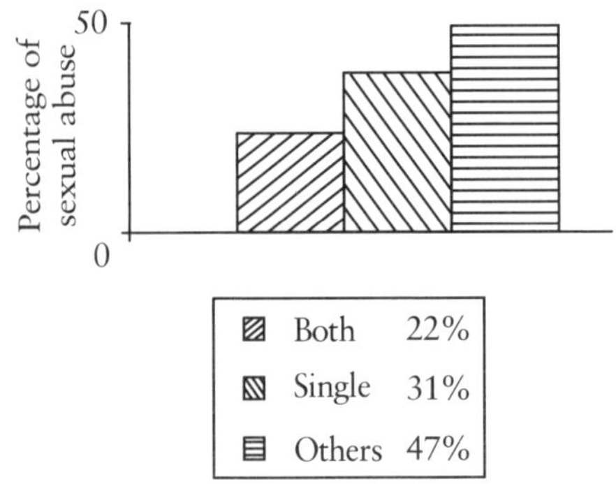

Both: Among children living with their own parents
Single: Among children living with single biological parent
Others: Among children living with caretakers and others

Emotional abuse in families where children live with both the parents was 26.3 per cent out of total emotionally abused children. In single parent type it was 32.5 per cent which was higher, and where the children live with others it was the highest, 41.2 per cent.

Emotional Abuse-Distribution According to Family Structure

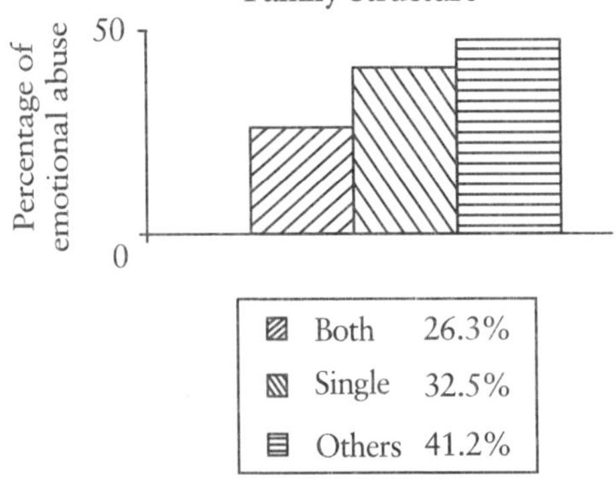

Both: Among children living with both the parents
Single: Among children living with single parent
Others: Among children living with others

In comparison with male children substance abuse was less in female children. The survey revealed that children living with single parent had the highest percentage of substance abuse. Those living with others had lesser chances of access to intoxicating substances than those who lived independently in hostels. The children living with both the parents were under lesser substance abuse than the other two category.

Substance Abuse-Distribution According to Family Structure

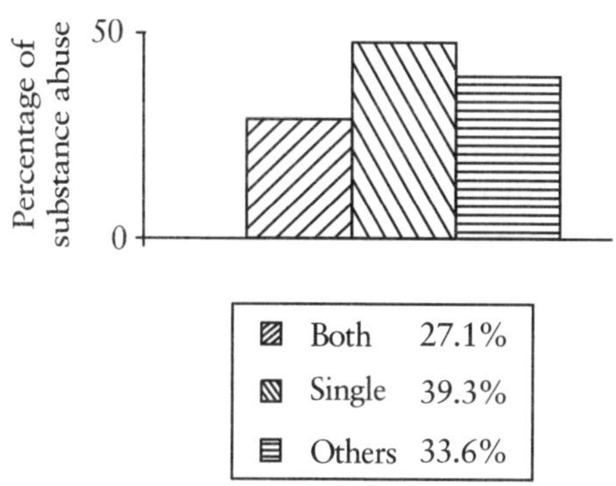

Both: Among children living with both the parents
Single: Among children living with single parent
Others: Among children living with others

In families where the children live with their own parents and grandparents neglect was the lowest. It was 19.20 per cent of the total neglected children. 36.6 per cent children living with single parent were estimated as being under neglect of different type. This is high rate of incidence. However, neglect was astonishingly high where children lived with others (54.2 per cent).

Neglect-Distribution According to Family Structure

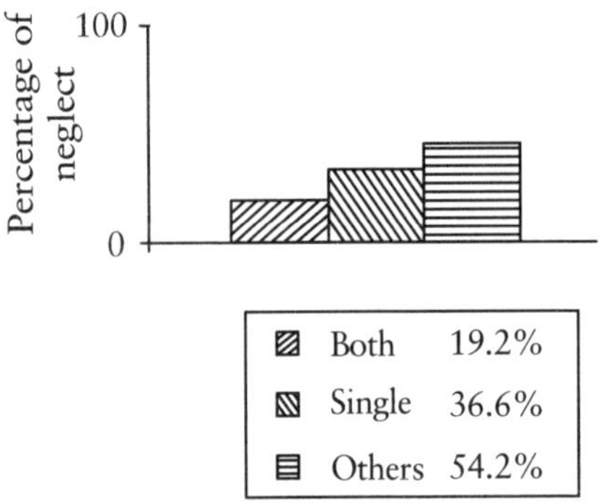

The children belonging to nuclear families suffer abuse even if they live with their own parents. However, it has been found that the rate goes down with those families where the grandparents are also present. Those living with single parent or under the care of 'others' suffer more neglect and abuse than those living with their own parents. In the elaborate set up of the joint family there was always one or other person to attend to the complaints of the child. 90 per cent of the adult respondents agreed that the joint family set up was the best environment for the growing child.

Number of Children in the Family and the Rate of Abuse

TABLE 2

Number of Children in Family and Rate of Abuse

Abuse category	Number of children in the family	Children abused (Out of 1000)
Total abuse	Only one	370
	Two	310
	Three and more	680
Total neglect	Only one	360
	Two	280
	Three and more	710

In families that have only one child have a higher rate of total abuse than those that have two children. There are various psycho-social factors that restrict abuse rate in two children family. Children from households with high incidence of neglect have high risk for sexual abuse outside home. When the number of children in the family goes up the rate of abuse and neglect increase. The table indicates that total abuse and total neglect are the highest in families with three or more children. When neglect at home increases children fall prey to perpetrators outside who at the moment have a hawk like attitude, they fall upon the easy prey, not properly cared for by the parents.

The highest incidence of child disappearance and sexual abuse were from those parts of Kerala with highest number of children per family—Malappuram. [According to the 2011 census Malappuram district has a population of 41,10,956, (which is 12.31 per cent of the State's population) roughly equal to the total population of Lebanon or the population of the US state of Oregon. This gives it a ranking of 50th in India (out of a total of 640). The district has a population density of 1,158 inhabitants per square kilometre (3,000/sq mi). Its population growth rate over the decade 2001-2011 was 13.39 per cent.] Survey among children and adolescents in the district has revealed that disappearance of children of both sex and child sexual abuse are rampant. Large scale sexual abuse of primary school children by the teachers too happen here. Although child vanishing is high here, according to the official records the district is only in the third position in the rank of disappearance of children.

Chart Indicating Total Disappearance in Each District*

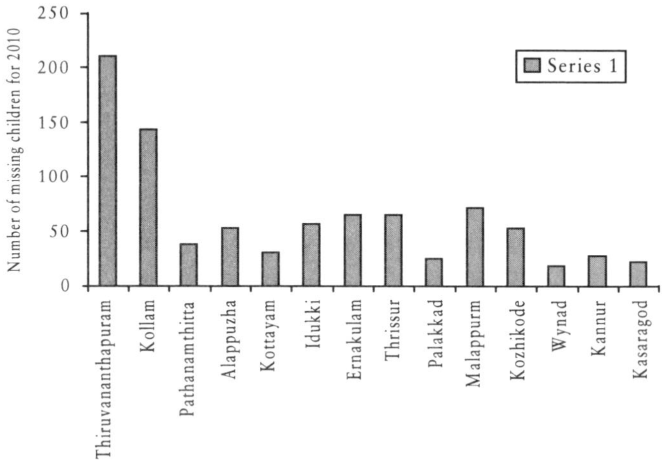

**Source*: State Crime Records Bureau.

The psychological structure of the family set up in Kerala is yet to undergo any drastic change. The physical and psychological structure of a family is not what it was forty years ago. Yet the complexities resulting out of a very loose structure where the parents escape responsibility which is characteristic of modern Western life is unapparent here. While a lot many families in Kerala have consciously restricted the number of children through birth control, a lot many have not yet found birth control a worthwhile practice. And we have found that the number of children in family influence maltreatment—the more the number of children in the family the more the chances of maltreatment and neglect. When compared with two child family the family with three or more children has a neglect rate which is very high and which increases steadily as the number of children increases. Therefore it is evident that a family of two children and two biological parents is a safe family if other aspects are not unfavourable.

Socio-cultural Aspects and Abuse

Researchers have noted that television cultivates exaggerated sense of danger and mistrust among regular viewers of crime—

sex-suspense dramas. The children are vulnerable to beliefs based on what they are visually and auditorily exposed to at a regular basis. They develop violence related fears, mistrust people, and tend to fancy becoming one they see on the screen. Television sends both auditory and visual impressions of make belief, of improbable or highly fanciful events, in a manner that captivates the young mind that is exposed to it on a regular basis. The impact is capable of turning the viewer suspicious of the very natural. There is then the tendency to believe and imitate the virtual. Rather than addressing itself to the nation's future the television system creates a culture outside reality.

During the survey in the state an astonishing number of children revealed that they view television for 4 to 6 hours a day. Most of them spend more time on watching television than on their studies. The children who made productive use of the television by watching news and educational programmes were few in comparison with those spending time on entertainment.

Time Children Spent on Watching Television

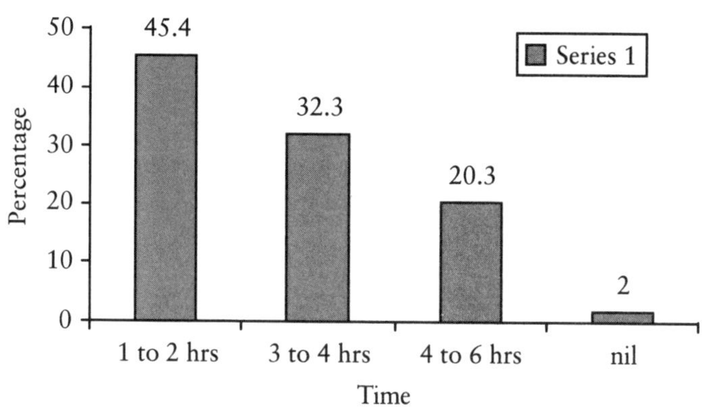

The adult respondents maintain that the time children spent on watching television, surfing internet, and using mobile phones has bred love for violence, bullying, alcoholism, early inducement into sexuality and sexual abuse of other children.

Opinion of Adults on Abuse Initiated by TV, Internet and Mobil Phones

43 per cent of the adult respondents believed that the regular child viewers of TV are more prone to violence than who are casual viewers. 36 per cent maintained that exposure to virtual reality was an inducement to sexual abuse of children by children. Everyday exposure to scenes of alcohol consumption breeds the habit of alcoholism on a large scale even in adults. 40 per cent of the respondents were of the view that the visual media enhanced alcoholism in children.

Tourism Related Sexual Abuse, Substance Abuse and Child Labour

The report on child abuse in the tourism sector (A Situational Analysis of Child Sex Tourism in Kerala and Goa, 2003), discusses abuse and paedophilia in Kovalam, Varkala, Kochi, and Kumaly. The report says that CST takes place in "unorganized settings or in legal establishments such as hotels".

> Most children interviewed have mentioned that they have had sex in places like hotels, lodges, street corners, beach, rooms where they live, deserted construction sites, etc.... Foreign tourists often use hotels, as it is the safest place as described by children for having sexual activities. Domestic tourists use small lodges and rooms in the bars for this purpose.

The present study has found that tourism related abuse is prevalent in Kumarakom, which is a tourist attraction in Kottayam district. The area which is a sensitive biosphere in ecological terms is a place where tourism is corrupting the eco-system and the system of human behaviour. Houseboats carrying tourists ply day and night on the back waters of Kumarakom.

Mr. Dipu of Kumarakom, who introduced himself as a researcher on the economics of tourism with reference to the changing economy of Kumarakom informed that there were more than 800 houseboats operating in Kumarakom area, and twenty resorts. The houseboats employ children, as there are no trained workers in this field. He maintained that child sexual abuse is part of tourism in this region. Kumarakom is "elite tourism" area (you don't see tourists wandering around as they are mostly in the houseboats, or on the lawns of resorts facing the lake watching the waves) as opposed to the "mass tourism" of Kovalam.

TABLE 3

Tourism Related Details from the Village of Kumarakom

Year	Number of foreign tourist visited Kumarakom[1]	Number of house boats at Kumarakom[2]	Number of resorts at Kumarakom Panchayat[3]	Number of 'homestays' at Kumarakom
2007	18,410	No official account	9 (official)	No account available
2008	20,567	—	10 (official)	,,
2009	21,690	—	11 (official)	,,
2010	22,620	176	11	,,

Source: 1. Department of Tourism. 2. Assistant Engineer, Canal Division, Alappuzha 3. Secretary, Kumarakom Panchayat

Number of foreigners who visited Kumarakom, a small 'raw' traditional village in Kottayam district, during the past four years.

Number of Tourists Visited Kumarakom 2007-2010

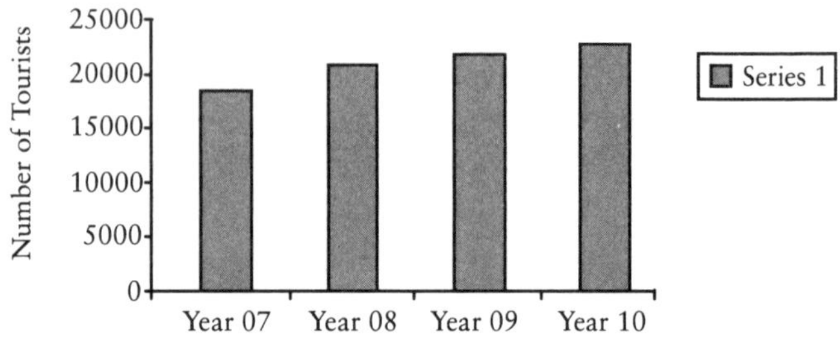

According to the tourism department 83,287 tourists visited Kumarakom between 2007 and 2010 the majority of them came from the UK and France. The official record showed only 176 houseboats on lake Vembanad in the Kumarakom area. According to Kumarakom Panchayat records, there were eleven resorts in its jurisdiction in 2010.

There are no rules regarding employment in the "house-boats" (modified indigenous wooden boats propelled by diesel engine). Naturally children provide cheap labour to the house-boat operators. In the night and even during the day time pedophiles have easy access to the victims because on the waters the police or the public do not notice what is happening under the thick bamboo-ply shelter of the houseboats. The boys are used as carriers of alcohol and even drugs to the house boats and resorts. In doing so they also develop the habit of deriving pernicious pleasure out of alcohol, drugs and sex. With so many houseboats on the lake with so many tourists, pollution is harmful not only to the natural environment but also to the human environment, in particular the child's environment.

In the light of the existing attitude to tourism as an industry to be promoted, what it costs to the life of children and the society that brings them up in the so-called tourist destinations has to be looked into. Why a greater awareness on the socio-cultural impact of tourism is necessary has been discussed by many a researcher in the field.

> Sexualities are integral to contemporary tourism, as are the social and economic structures within which those

> representations and transactions take place.... Issues of rape and assault are also increasingly related to tourism while campaigns against sex tourism, and child sex tourism in particular have also created greater awareness in tourism generating regions that the relationship between sex and tourism is not either romantic or beneficial to the destination. (Ryan and Hall, 2001: Preface)

The data on child sex tourism and abuse at Kumarakom were collected from local people, children below 18 years and schoolteachers. It was not easy for truth to come out because the local people although not very happy about what was (and is) happening to their society, appeared to be apprehensive while the researcher made an attempt to get at the core of what was happening to them. The researcher noticed while attempting to interview children at private aided schools in Kumarakom, that their teachers had warned them not to answer too private questions, which implied that there were truths to hide. However, in Government Schools the teachers were open which made it easier for the researcher to identify the victims among the children. One of the teachers supplied evidence to pedophilia by foreign tourists.

Of the total children interviewed at Kumarakom tourist destination, one-third had abusive experiences of the physical and sexual kind at the resorts, houseboats and home stays. The children who were victims of substance abuse were mostly boys who acted as carriers of intoxicating substances to those who spend their holidays at the resorts and houseboats. In the houseboats the boys were used to perform menial jobs like washing and cleaning, bring things to the tourists and also to gratify their sexual needs. The boys themselves consumed intoxicating substances like alcohol and ganja whenever there was an opportunity. Thus the boys were victims of pedophilia by foreign tourists, and the girls on the other hand fell victim to sexual abuse. It was therefore apparent that physical, sexual and substance abuse were rampant at Kumarakom at the time of data collection.

In the three abuse locations identified, out of the total abused, 39.6 per cent was physical abuse, 30.4 per cent sexual abuse and 30 per cent substance abuse.

Abuse locations:

- Resorts
- Houseboats
- Home stays

Distribution of Abuse (at Resorts, Home Stays and in Houseboats)

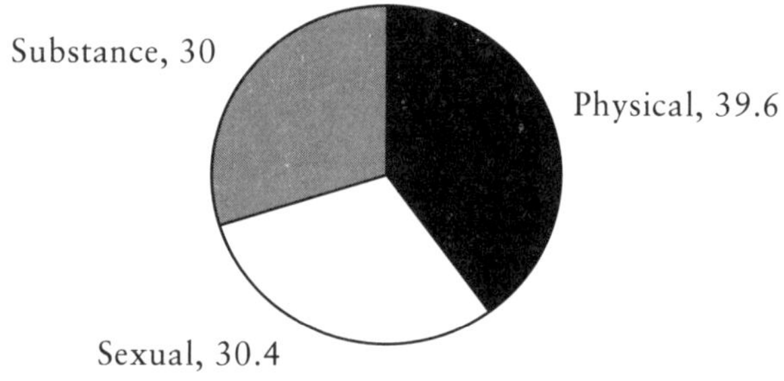

The indigenous population of Kumarakom, who have been farmers, farm labourers, fishers, 'toddy-tappers', or employees in the local toddy shop in the context of the report, experience commoditization of their lives at the emergence of the tourist as the consumer. People find working for the tourism industry, whatever the work might be, more profitable than engaging in locally available income generating work. They therefore look at the tourist as a source of easy income. A school-employee in Kumarakom said that many children who leave home for school do not reach school, but get into profit making by doing menial jobs or catering to the sexual needs of a foreign tourist. This gives him/her the money they need to squander. For the tourist at Kumarakom as elsewhere, the destination is an escape from the routine life. The indigenous Keralites to most of them are commodities that can satisfy their hedonistic needs. The tourist therefore purchases the service of a child, male or female. The resorts of Kumarakom to the natives, are holiday homes that generate income. The houseboats are not vehicles that carry the tourist through their waterways exposing him/her to the beauty of the canopied little islands, but income generating appliances. That to the tourist, both—the resort and the houseboat—are places of entertainment or even brothels could be truth from another angle. Some adult respondents belonging to this region were apprehensive of the influence of tourism on the children's approach to life—even parents being viewed in terms of the cash they possessed. They are apprehensive of the gradual loss of the sense of identity of the entire community—the children who are victims of tourist sex abuse, and the people who temporarily benefit out of tourism industry might become culturally disoriented, their identity under crisis, the effect of which might eventually swallow the rest.

The Perpetrator

9

It appears from the present rate of child abuse, especially child sexual abuse in this part of the country, that almost any person can turn an abuser. Anyone who has seen the social life of Kerala three decades ago will smell the difference. Due to excessive exposure to the virtual world, many children are not able to perceive the real, and the same is working on many adults who think that it isn't bad to use a child for his/her benefit even if it is detrimental to the child. It is not that a child of our definition cannot abuse another child. The abuser can be of any age, who is physically and mentally capable of committing the act.

The abuser can be the child's parent, caretaker, sibling, relative, friend, an employee of the child's household, or someone at the child's place of work. The abuser could also be the child's stepfather or stepmother, adoptive parents, or those at the orphanage if the child is an orphan. For neglect to happen, the perpetrator must be a person responsible to the child's growth.

The abuser could be:

Parents

Grandparents

Stepfather/stepmother

Adoptive parents

Other relatives

Male/female friends of the parents

Caretakers

Neighbours

Teachers

Employer

Others at the place of employment

Others including strangers

TABLE 1

Abuser Category and the Percentage of Harm Done

Type	Abuser	% of Children Abused
Total abuse	Parents and relatives	56
	Caretakers	22
	Others	22
Physical abuse	Parents and relatives	68
	Caretakers	20
	Others	12
Emotional abuse	Parents and relatives	70
	Caretakers	20
	Others	10
Sexual abuse	Parents and relatives	30
	Caretakers	26
	others	44
Neglect	Parents and relatives	88
	Caretakers	12

Physical abuse mostly happens at the child's home and the perpetrators are in good number the parents and/or relatives. The same is the case with emotional abuse. In fact emotional abuse perpetrated by parents and close relatives come at the top of abuse that happens at home. Sexual abuse too happens at home. But in the majority of incidents the abuse is not directly initiated by the parents, but rather it happens due to parental neglect. Most perpetrators of sexual abuse are "others" who include even the child's friends, parents of friends, teachers and strangers. Since neglect can happen only when a responsible person does not realize, or deliberately moves away from his/her responsibility to the child, others do not come in this category. Neglect happens where the child lives and that for most part is a lapse or error on the part of the parents. So, most perpetrators of neglect are the child's own parents.

There are circumstances when the same child is abused by more than one perpetrator. Neglect too can be of one or more type. Maintaining an attitude that is not conducive to the proper growth of the child and denying medical care when it is essential are physical neglect. If this comes from parents or care-takers they are the perpetrators. If the same perpetrator abuses differently, for example the child is physically and sexually abused by the same person, s/he is a more dangerous perpetrator than one who indulges in a single abuse. At the time of assessing as to who could the immediate perpetrator be the answer was 'the parent' or one who was very close to the child.

An important observation regarding child abuse by others, especially of the sexual kind, is about the teachers, who in trust must come second to the parents. They were found to be the worst sexual abusers in some parts of Kerala, especially Malappuram district where primary school children, in particular male children, were sexually abused in large numbers—by male teachers of Government, aided, self-financing, and even religious schools. From the sheer number of the abused, it appears to the researcher that the perpetrators belonging to a particular social group especially in the northern districts of Kerala seem to believe that there is nothing wrong in making children belonging to both sexes, objects of their sexual gratification. The testimony by children indicate that the perpetrators ensnare them with the help of pornographic clips on mobile phone. This shows that neither lack of education, nor lack of employment, nor economic insufficiency alone cause abuse. There is something more than that. And that lies deep-rooted in the individual psyche and the consciousness of the social group.

The Unkindest Cut of All

When a fatal abuse occurs from a trusted hand, as Mark Antony declares in Shakespeare's *Julius Caesar*, it is the 'unkindest cut of all', severest of abuse the child might suffer. Perhaps many do not know that in the state of Kerala the children face severe abuse at their own home. The same hands that once fed honey and *acoras calamus* (in Malayalam *thenum vayambum*—honey and the medicinal root that is fed to the new born) dole out the worst as the child grows. That the educated and uneducated vie each other in maltreatment signify that education has failed to teach restraint, and love and respect for everything living, not to speak of to who one is directly responsible. The highest rate of emotional abuse (70 per cent), the highest rate of physical abuse (68 per cent) and neglect (88 per cent) are meted out to the children by those who are directly responsible to the child's welfare, like the parents and very near relations. That the child in Kerala has to face or fear even sexual abuse at his/her own home (30 per cent), or he/she suspects his/her parents on that account reveal a high degree of lack of trust at home. This lack of trust breeds disharmony and causes break up which shall have wider consequences.

However, many testimonies by children warrant that slaps on the face and blows from parents are not as hard or injurious as the same received from others. When a caretaker slaps a child on the face or kicks him/her he could be merciless and brutal. Moreover, fatal physical tortures like burns are not attempted by parents. (An incident of fatal injuries including burns leading to the death of a fourteen-year-old domestic help girl in Ernakulam district is cited elsewhere in this study.)

The above findings indicate that during the period of dependency from early childhood till the age of eighteen, the children experience different types of maltreatment from their family. The responses from adult respondents concerning the causes of the abusive adult behaviour are shown in Table 2.

In normal family situations it is the mother in the house that punishes the children more. But that becomes severe only occasionally. And when the father does the same it is more severe. However, it isn't the case where there is only one natural parent present. When there is a stepfather or stepmother, it is the stepfather whose maltreatment is frequent and more severe. Stepmothers indulge more in emotional abuse, whereas stepfathers perpetrate physical, emotional and sexual abuse. A child testimony from Malappuram district is given (cf. Annex 1) to prove that even when the single parent is the child's biological father, sexual abuse by him can happen. (At Parappanagady, Malappuram, a Upper Primary School teacher, A.K. Ashraf, was nabbed by Parappanagady Police under the Juvenile Justice Act for large scale sexual abuse of the children of his school. After a team of counselors had conducted counseling for the students for two days, it came out that fifty male children of class V and VI were sexually maltreated by this teacher. The children were ensnared with the help of pornographic clips on mobile phone. This, however, happened in November 2011, after the data collection was over. Sexual abuse of school children is widespread in Malappuram district. The researcher has the feeling that a good many adults in this part of the state seem to believe that they have a right to sexually abuse children because they themselves grew up in an abusive environment.)

TABLE 2

Child Abuse at Home (Excluding Neglect)—Adult Responses Regarding Causes and Impact

Type of abuse	Perpetrator	Causes identified by adult respondents	Nature of impact on the abused identified
Total abuse	Adults in the family	Nuclear family, broken family, changing attitude to life, financial constraints, stress, influence of media and internet	Serious physical and psychological impairment
Physical abuse	1. Male parent and male relatives	Tension, financial problems, alcoholism, personality disorders, occupational stress, laxity	Serious to moderate physical injury, may develop aggressiveness and lack of concern moderate

Type of abuse	Perpetrator	Causes identified by adult respondents	Nature of impact on the abused identified
	2. Female parent and relatives	Tension, incompatibility, financial problems, laxity, occupational stress	physical injury
Emotional abuse	Both parents and relatives	All of the above	Serious to moderate growth impairment, lack of confidence, indifference, hate and distrust
Sexual abuse	1. Parents and close relatives	Personality disorders, alcoholism and drug addiction, lack of moral education	Serious to moderate impairment to growth, personality disorders
	2. Other relatives	Lack of moral education, depression, absence of parental supervision due to neglect or inability	

Taking total abuse into account it is found that the children endure more from their biological parents. Of the two, father and mother, the mother tops in total abuse with 70 per cent and father next with 56 per cent. However, 62 per cent of stepfathers and 45 per cent of stepmothers are abusive.

A complex problem like the one under examination often defies accuracy because the input received may not often be accurate. Yet the inputs have to be relied and this is a limitation to this study. According to the data available the majority of the perpetrators of child abuse are between the age of 26 and 60.

Age of the Abuser and Share of Total Abuse

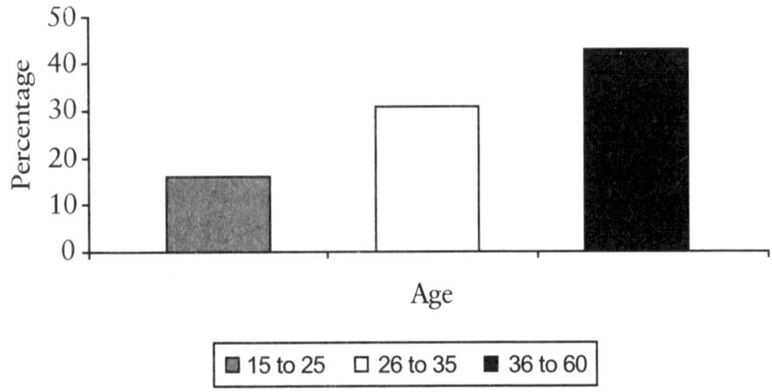

Between the age of 15 and 25 lesser tendency to be abusive was noticed because only 16 per cent of this age group was identified as abusive—a sizeable portion of this belonged to certain community in the north of Kerala. Between the age of 26 and 35 there was increasing tendency to be abusive. 31 per cent belonging to this group were found to be abusive. Between 35 and 60 abuse rate was very high, as 43 per cent of the abusers identified belonged to this group.

Findings and Conclusions 10

This study has relied mostly on the information received from the children and the stakeholders. The reports on child abuse appearing presently in daily newspapers and the electronic media warrant the validity of the analysis. The glossy image of Kerala society that was in the limelight was blurred by the findings regarding the serious state of child abuse that was revealed in the report of 2007, which covered only two districts of the State. The present report opens to view a more ashen picture.

The Government of India has taken steps to find solutions to the problem through various laws enacted from time to time. These steps have to yet prove themselves valid. Although this is not a study that has scanned every nook and corner of Kerala to extract facts about the problem, the available data suggest the existence of an unhappy atmosphere as far as the state of affairs of the children are concerned.

National Policy for Children, 1974, upheld the nation's children as a "supremely important asset". However, the report published by the Ministry of Women and Child Development in 2007 (Study on Child Abuse: India 2007) calls the situation of children in India "alarming" which means that there are causes for people to worry about their children and which also means that the declaration of 1974—children as a supremely important asset—did not carry the weight of execution. Recently various NGOs, doctors and government officials who deal with the problem in the state have unequivocally called the situation of children problematic which needs a planned approach. Nuclear family, increase in the consumption of alcohol, the tendency to give priority to things of pleasure and comfort, subordination of values to personal gains, the misuse of electronic contrivances like TV, mobile phone and computer (internet) have become topics of arm chair discussions on child abuse at least in select circles. Everyone who reads newspapers say that there is a problem. But their thoughts on abuse are not very serious even at this moment.

The increase in the rate of abuse in the State, especially sexual abuse, after the first official attempt at data collection in 2004 signify the undesirable and unhealthy changes happening in the Kerala society. Although the work of voluntary organizations in this area has been in the offing and awareness programmes are conducted here and there, these attempts are barely sufficient to halt the unhealthy traits that have permeated into the individual and the society.

Whatever programmes have been initiated have been for the better. The state has the highest literacy rate in India. For the time being, there is decline in poverty and increase in employment. This, however, is no indicator to over all development. The state of affairs unravelled in this project show the murky side of early 21st century Kerala. Violence in the family is on the increase, break up of relations frequent. There hasn't been any sincere attempt on the part of the State Government to contain the threat accompanying the increasing consumption of alcohol. The causes behind the distressing increase of sexual abuse in the state deserve in depth study.

The study has looked into the various inducements to the problem. A close analysis of the financial position of the family, family history, the nature of the occupation of the parents, family structure, family atmosphere and interpersonal relationship at one level and an exhaustive study of the present social set-up that surrounds the family at the other, can evolve a clearer picture of the problem.

This study has attempted to include children belonging to different strata of Kerala society. This was ascertained with the help of the income of the child's family, the education of the parent/parents, and his/her/their job and also whether or not the child himself/herself was a wage earner. The majority of the samples were school going children, especially those in government and aided schools. A characteristic of the children in government schools in the south of Kerala is that they mostly belong to the lower income families and in the north they represent a cross section that includes the poor and the economically advantageous alike. The entire lot, however represented children from different socio-economic background.

Physical abuse, emotional abuse and neglect are widespread in low income group families. Their predicament and the incidence of abuse among them were apparent in direct observation. However, that wasn't the case with higher income families. (Generally abuse in these families are masked, not immediately perceptible. This obscurity, however, is lost when the child discloses his 'experiences' to the counselor or teacher.) Teachers and counselors could give important evidence to the researcher. Abuse in higher income families was assessed in this mode.

A significant concern during data collection was the complexity and difficulty associated with it. External sources that provide appropriate data are lacking. Police, Department of Child Welfare and Childline are active, but do not have proper ways of providing accurate data for research. An all inclusive approach that can deal with the problem is not there at the moment. There are quite a number of limitations to the proper recording of data concerning physical abuse, sexual abuse and emotional abuse and neglect.

Since in Kerala 91.98 per cent women and 96.02 per cent men are literate (according to the 2011 census) it is obvious that 90 per cent or more children reach schools. As things stand, an estimation of the rate of abuse, its intensity, and the damage it causes to the children could be carried out with the help of samples from schools in different districts of the state. An abuse monitoring cell in each school can identify abuse and compile data. But at present such an arrangement does not exist in the schools. If there is one it will be a good way out where teachers themselves indulge in large scale sexual abuse. During the investigation it was found that in schools, corporal punishment was less in comparison with the school days of the sixties. However, teachers indulging in large scale sexual abuse of young children is an entirely new phenomenon in the state. The uncertainty and doubt that has wrapped up the education sector due to numerous factors the predominant among which is commoditization of the individual, and the superabundance of private schools that function according to the ideology of the market, have cut down the teachers' loyalty and dedication. In the absence of an abuse monitoring cell the researcher had to rely on the child's immediate response as the marker of what happened to him/her at school and home. This in the present context is a deterrent to proper data collection on abuse from schools.

The study did not exactly measure the intensity of impact of abuse on the child. However, it was found that familial, academic and social situations are not conducive to the physical, emotional and intellectual well being of the child. The situation is alarming because it can shatter the body and mind of the society of the region in the not too distant future.

The situation of children exposed by the study demands genuine social awareness of the problem. The researcher did meet individuals who were complacent enough to believe that child abuse of the magnitude indicated cannot happen in the state. The parents are the most responsible to the child. The study did bring to the fore serious flaws in the attitude of the parents that cause the development of a corresponding attitude in the child which decidedly affects his or her future in the wrong way. Alcoholism which is on the increase in the state has its influence on the child at home and at school. Exposure to obscenity and violence on the television and pornography on the mobile and internet, along with the tendency to find pleasure in intoxicants have created an evil atmosphere without precedent.

The parents were found complaining that they didn't have sufficient time to attend to the needs of the child. The number of employed mothers have increased. Smaller children of employed parents in the nuclear family set-up were left with day care centres that were barely sufficient to cater everything the infant needs. Another important finding regarding child rearing was the impatience shown by mothers. Most of the mothers reported to the researcher that their children were more demanding than they (the parents) had been as children.

Good many parents of school going children wanted the schools to take care of them. In the State the number of schools with ill paid and ill trained teachers are on the increase. The parents pay high amounts to private schools that offer extra care for their children in return. But in fact these schools mostly have ill-trained and ill-paid teachers. (The public school system is not in a healthy situation.)

Legislations to contain abuse shall become effective to some extent if there are sufficient and repeated awareness programmes consecutively for at least five years. Moral and aesthetic education is on the decline in the state. Traditional values are seldom taught at schools. Compulsory education of the indigenous tradition, history and art and the morals the tradition upheld along with codes of conduct for teachers, students and parents shall bring the highly essential restraint needed in the times. Respect for one's own self shall grow alongside respect for others and the environment.

In certain parts of the State there exists a deplorable state of sexuality in males. From the enormity of the instances of child sexual abuse from the northern districts of Malappuram and Kasaragod it could be deduced that it is socially sanctioned to some extent. Moralising may not work in such perpetrators. Therefore, strict enforcement of the laws pertaining to the sexual abuse of children are necessary especially in the 'hot spots' mentioned.

This researcher's contention is that appointment of teachers at schools should be made only after strictly assessing their attitude to children and their growth. The presence of a child friendly and patriotic psychologist is necessary at every school up to the twelfth standard.

The State should put control on alcohol consumption and an absolute check on the availability of narcotics substances.

The individualist/individualism has entered into the social life of Kerala. The individualist furthers his or her own interests, or at least demands the right to serve his or her own interests, without taking the interests of society into consideration. Earlier the society used to give credence to a philosophy that requires the sacrifice of the self-interest of the individual for any higher social causes. The individualism which is reigning the society of Kerala is the twin brother of anarchism or liberalism. The immediate identifiable indicators are the increasing craze for money and pleasure; lack of restraint and tolerance and lack of respect for other individuals. Exposure to excesses on internet and mobile phone; alcoholism and drug addiction, watching TV dramas and near porn advertisements have furthered this. Individualism appears to have gained upper hand pushing down collective interest: self-centredness has taken over, which means turning one's back on the values which were hitherto considered eternal. This is a fertile ground for abuse, where the weak are the easy victims. Direct result—child sexual abuse betray exponential growth in Kerala.

Economic liberalization that the Government of India has introduced after 1991 has enabled clever people to make money at faster paces. In the State of Kerala a number of people enjoying the fruits of new opportunities in the market have shown a tendency to escalate the feelings of the common people for money and comfort through lavish spending on luxury. While squandering money and extravaganza are common with some people, it is not a rare event that they turn powerful and corrupt and invite others to corruption. Those who at the moment witness the mindless extravaganza appear to have under the influence taken turns even to frenzy-bidding farewell to values and relationship.

The inauspicious traits of the neo-liberal interests of the State are apparent in the manner in which the hopes and aspirations of the people have been diverted. There is an under world empire operating with a capital of more than fifty lakh crores in Kerala who need the week to be cheated. They plan their agenda to have this need met.

Three million years of natural selection in the course evolution of the human species has ingrained in human nature the instinct to nurture their offsprings. If natural selection is a valid concept, infant nurturing lies deep in human nature. The human child has a long infancy which it cannot manage on its own; only those children whose parents are nurturant and supportive shall survive (Albee George W. 1980:115-16). This being fact, all attempts at child abuse are unnatural. Excessive power of some sort is behind every form of stress and distress. "... On a more personal level the exploitation of women by men, of children by adults, of the elderly by the youth worshiping society—it is enough to suggest the hypothesis that a dramatic reduction and control of power might improve the mental health of people" (Kessler and Albee, 1975). The contention here is that abuse is ultimately the externalization of a mental faculty that has been malfunctioning.

Father and mother, whose accountability is absolute in the physical and mental well-being of the children have traditionally been placed along with guru and god. For the consumerist society, every thing including a child is a commodity. Moral duty is subordinate to the cravings of the body, it is less significant, therefore the adults who are parents seem to have stepped down from the high pedestal. Politicians who were erstwhile champions of the poor have turned out to be opportunists who would not miss a chance to abuse an unfortunate girl. This gives out that poverty is not the only reason for abuse. This necessitates that moral and aesthetic education be made compulsory part of school and college education.

Popularity of internet porn, indiscriminate display of nudity on television, loss of faith in virtues, the thought that there is nothing called morality are factors influencing life in Kerala. Alcohol and drugs affecting vital systems, chemically treated food, polluted air and water affecting the nervous system, loss of sleep, loss of ethical consideration, and the thought that money can buy prestige, comfort and pleasure have generated a socially toxic environment in the state.

A large scale abuse of school children is possible and only later will the incident come to the notice of the concerned. The vulnerability is enhanced by the general feeling created by the visual media and careless parents. In many schools in Kerala, there are gangs of bullies who physically, sexually and emotionally abuse weaker children. They make them watch porn movie clips on mobile phone and offer them intoxicants before sexually abusing them. They demand money and physically assault children who defy them.

When the physical environment of an individual of average mental disposition is polluted there is every chance of his becoming abusive, because his own senses are abused.

Policies adopted by the government from time to time are less effective because of the inherent defects. And the defects could be traced back to the larger corruption that Indians have gradually accepted as part of life.

Major findings of the Study:

- Abuse rate is more among boys than among girls.
- Child sex abuse is rampant in the State.
- Boys are more sexually abused than girls.
- Every second child was abused in the state during the period of study.
- In the State of Kerala one out of every third child suffer at least one agonizing kind of abuse.
- 44.36 per cent children suffered physical abuse.
- 39.30 per cent were sexually abused.
- 13.23 per cent were subjected to substance abuse.
- 57 per cent were found to experience emotional abuse during the survey.
- Of the total emotionally abused children in the family set-up, 39.4 per cent had drunkard abusers.
- 52 per cent were found to be under neglect.
- Abuse rate is increasing irrespective of high literacy.

- The majority of the perpetrators of child abuse were between the age of 26 and 60.
- The possibility of abuse at the hands of parents and relatives is high.
- The social environment of the State is not safe for the children.
- Even though the total number of births in the State has decreased, the rate of incidence of child abuse has gone up.
- The State is, according to the findings, a less safe place for its children, according to the standards of safety outlined in the definition of abuse in this study.
- Child rearing by adults and child behaviour towards adults have changed radically resulting in circumstances that are not conducive to the well-being of children and the society that these children will make later in their life.
- The social environment in the State is conducive to abuse.
- Speaking about different forms of abuse is still a taboo in the State.
- Increased alcohol consumption has enhanced child abuse. Consumption of alcohol has almost become a fashion among children in the school final and higher secondary stage.
- Electronic media, internet and mobile phones have widened the possibility of child abuse.
- The amount spent on liquor in Kerala if constructively employed in creating employment for the unemployed, can, apart from nourishing the society in other ways, reduce the present rate of child maltreatment.
- Because the number of drinking adults have gone up at an exponential rate children in the State are more at risk now.
- At the moment in the State one out of every three children suffers drug and alcohol caused abuse.

- Unpleasant homes drive children towards easy money making and pleasure hunt.
- Lack of proper education leading to proper awareness, the limitations of the individual, and the infatuation for luxury goods and intoxicating substances which is the outcome of neo-liberalism have escalated the lay individual's tendency to abuse.
- Lure of comfort and luxury accompanied by premature exposure to sexuality through the electronic media and neglect on the part of parents or caretakers prepare ground for an easy glide into the hands of racketeers.
- When the number of children in the family goes up the rate of abuse and neglect also goes up.
- Total abuse and total neglect were the highest in families with three or more children. When neglect at home increased, children fell prey to perpetrators outside who had a hawk like attitude (they fall upon the easy prey, not properly cared for by the parents.)
- It was found that a family of two children and two biological parents was a safe family if other aspects were not unfavourable.
- The time children spent on watching television, surfing internet, and using mobile phones has induced love for violence, bullying, alcoholism, early inducement into sexuality and sexual abuse of other children.

Annexures

ANNEXURE I

Testimony by Children (a few samples)

- An eleven-year old, girl, belonging to a poor family from a village in the east of Kottayam district said: "My mother beats me severely accusing mischief. I was very upset and could not hold on. I wanted to commit suicide by jumping into the artesian well nearby. The next day was the Christmas day. I told my decision to my elder sister."
- Rural girl, economically backward, eleven year old, Kottayam District: "I was watching TV. My mother came in furiously and beat me. Those were exam days. I am a good student. Then, why should she beat me so mercilessly for watching television?"
- Eleven-year old, poor, rural girl, Kottayam district: "Our basic sciences teacher beat me one day. I was very sad and upset. It seemed nobody would console me. Yet there was a friend. She said soothing words."
- Eleven-year old, poor, rural girl: "One day my father thrashed me and asked me questions which I did not answer. I was horrified. He continued beating me. Now I hate the very sight of him."
- Twelve-year old, rural, poor, girl: "One day I pushed down my younger sister. Furious at the sight my father thrashed me very hard. Skin had ripped off my left calf muscle and it developed into a pus filled wound. I began hating my father and mother. But my hate is ebbing away slowly."

- Twelve-year old, poor, rural boy: "I was watching television with my friend. Seeing my father returning from work for lunch, I closed the door. The door hit my father's leg. Out of anger he beat me severely and threw me on the ground."
- Seventeen-year old boy from Kumarakom Panchayat in Kottayam district, son of a toddy tapper, who is a class X student said that he was being harmed psychologically by people he wouldn't name. He finds employment in the resorts and has acquainted himself with foreign tourists. He said that in the preceding month he consumed liquor approximately eight times. He has a mobile phone and also engages in internet chat. He also said that he knew several children in his locality who work in the tourism area and lead a similar life.
- Another seventeen-year old boy from the same locality with similar background said that he was under mental pressure. He admitted having been sexually abused. He has consumed liquor and hashish.
- A fifteen-year old boy, son of a daily wage earner belonging to Kumarakom said that he was physically and mentally harmed by others. At school he was bullied. He has watched pornographic movie clips with his friends. A friend of his had sexually abused him which he didn't reveal to his parents. When he is sad, there is nobody to console him.
- Sixteen-year old boy belonging to Aymanem in Kottayam district said that he knew tourists from abroad; he has consumed hallucinogen and he has been sexually abused, which he did not tell anyone.
- A sixteen-year old girl belonging to Arpukkara Panchyat in Kottayam district disclosed that she was victim of sexual abuse. She was molested by strangers. She also said that she has used opiates like hashish, LSD and morphine.
- A sixteen-year old boy from Thiruvarpu, Kottayam said that he was bullied at school. He was shown porn

movie by his brother. He has acquainted himself with foreign tourists. He visits the internet café of his locality and has a mobile phone which he uses to send messages and watch porn clips.

- A fourteen-year old boy, son of a casual labourer at Kumarakom Panchayat in Kottayam district, class IX student at the local school said: "I am beaten at home. Yet I manage to watch TV three hours a day. I am bullied and insulted at school by the bullies in my class. I have carried liquor to others for which I was paid. I own a mobile phone; I have watched obscene movies and was sexually abused. I haven't disclosed these matters to my parents."
- A fourteen-year old boy, class IX student at a Govt. school in Kollam town said: "My parents are casual workers. I was bullied and robbed at school by the student 'goondas'. A neighbour used to sexually abuse me which I have disclosed to my parents and a friend."
- A sixteen-year old boy belonging to a lower middle class family of Thrikkadavoor, in Kollam district, class IX student, said: "At school I am bullied and tortured by a bully. He demands money from me and wants to sexually abuse me. I have been asked to carry intoxicants for others. I have been sexually abused at home when my parents were absent, I have been shown porn movie clips by a friend and was even photographed nude. I was afraid of making a complaint to my parents or to the police, but I have revealed this to another friend of mine."
- Fifteen-year old boy, son of a casual labourer, living in Kollam town reported: "At school I am physically tortured by a bully called Job. He is my class leader. He gives me blows when he is annoyed. At home I have been sexually approached by a relative. Job has shown me porn movie clips and has taken my nude photograph and has used me sexually. I was afraid of telling this to others. Sometimes I go to work to earn some money."

- A fourteen-year old girl belonging to Katdhinamkulam Panchayat of Thiruvananthapuram district said: "My parents are carpenters. They are very authoritative. They want me to reach a good position in life. However, they scarcely help in my studies. I have furtively drunk beer and have seen porn clips on mobile phone."
- A fourteen-year old girl belonging to Madappally village, Kottayam district said: "At home my father drinks alcohol, my five-year-old brother imitates him. My father comes home drunk in the evening and insults me physically and mentally. Sometimes I experience great tension. I was sexually assaulted by a relative. I disclosed this to my mother, but nothing happened. I have been asked by my father and one relative to buy narcotic substances from sellers. I myself have used morphine."
- A thirteen-year old girl living in Thiruvalla Municipality in Pathanamthitta district confessed that she was being mentally tortured. She had been a victim of insulting behaviour by a neighbour. The parents are not able to give her confort. She said that she finds comfort in her own self. Her father who came home in the evening was often drunk and wouldn't hesitate to throw an insult or two at her.
- A fifteen-year old boy belonging to Elamkkara in Kochi, Ernakulam disrict (who is only one among the many like him in this part of the State I met) said, "My father is a driver and my mother is a nurse. When they leave, I and my sister, are left at home without care. We are both students. My parents like my sister more. To me their attitude is that of unconcern. There is nobody to help me in my studies. However there is no shortage of blows. I like a friend of mine more than I like my parents. I have consumed liquor and narcotics, the other month I took six seals of marijuana. I have also acted as a carrier of liquor to other persons. I am used to watching porn clips on mobile phone and computer

and have been abused sexually by a friend, a cousin and others."

- A sixteen-year old girl, tenth class student at the HMYHS (Yathim Ghana HS) at Manjeri, Malappuram district, revealed her plight in this manner. "My mother died a year and a half ago. I am under the care of my maternal uncle and aunt. The aunt and the uncle behave as if they are not interested in my affairs. At home I suffer great tension. The house and the surroundings give me no comfort. I am tortured physically and mentally. I am afraid of the people around. However, the teachers are considerate. My father misbehaves with me when others are not at home. He gives an uncomfortable stare whenever, I am alone which makes me uneasy and nervous. I have been shown obscene pictures and porn videos by my father. He has asked me to touch his private body parts. Several times he kissed me in the sexual manner. I haven't disclosed this to anyone because I am afraid of doing so."
- An eighteen-year old adolescent boy belonging to Chambakkulam in Kuttanad, Alappuzha said he would do anything if he is paid for that. He is educated (HSE) and runs a tea stall in the night to pull on himself and his brother. When this researcher asked whether he could kill somebody for money, he answered in the affirmative.

Adjunct

- In May 2012, a fifteen-year old boy, student of class nine at Muttar St. George Higher Secondary School in Muttar, Pathanamthitta district, drove a knife through his friend's neck leaving him dead in the backyard of the school. When the police caught him the next day, he confessed that the crime was the result of a petty quarrel between him and the boy he killed. He conducted the 'operation' in the manner of 'Rambo', a Western movie character. The boy is a mother forsaken child who lives with his father who lives with his fourth wife. The killer child said that he hates everyone except himself.

Adult Respondents on Child Abuse

- A thirty-two year old adult belonging to Kumarakom, Kottayam said, "The children are growing selfish. They don't value relationship. Tourism mesmerizes children and enhances sexual activities in them. (Kumarakom is an example). We have to be watchful".
- A forty-nine year old male from Kumarakam said "The children in the state have been wrongly influenced by tourism and the electronic media. The coming of the tourists have a morally weakening influence on the children. They drift away from values. The children are incapable of understanding the difference between western values and ours. They learn alcoholism from the family and friends."
- A thirty-seven year old woman from Kumarakom said "The children imbibe wrong things from the computer software and the internet and try to practise what they see." She also maintained that the attitude to the child and childhood in Kerala is on the decline despite high rate of literacy.
- A forty-two year old woman, teacher of mathematics at a private school at Kumarakom said: "From the television and internet the children learn wrong things and they tread the wrong path."
- A forty-three year old woman from Kumarakom, Kottayam said: "Interaction between parents and children is becoming rare. They spent more time on mobiles and internet and watching the channels. Neither the parents nor the teachers are worried about erosion of moral values."
- A forty-five year old Government H.S. teacher at Kumarakom said, "Kumarakom is a tourist destination. There are plenty of resorts at Kumarakom. It has been

found that children belonging to financially poor households become easy prey to sexual abuse. We [the teachers at this school] have recently questioned three tenth standard boys who confessed sexual encounters with foreign tourists at the resorts at Kumarakom."

- At Kumarakom Panchayat which is the hub of tourism in Kottayam district the researcher found that local people rent a part of their house to foreign tourists and earn a good amount of money in that way. The children go as tourist guides in houseboats, sell themselves and earn money. Some children who are more industrious go on fishing during holidays.
- Mr. Suresh, a govt. employee who the researcher met at Kumarakom said that tourism in Kumarakom has become a means of illegitimate activities. In the houseboats there are no proper employees. They use children—both school going and those who do not attend schools—to do all the jobs. Some of them get attracted to the immoral activities that the tourists indulge inside the houseboat. They are used as buyers of IMFL from the outlets of Beverages corporation for use by the tourists in the houseboats. For whatever, they do in the house boat, the children are paid more than they expect. And they begin to enjoy wine and women at a tender age.
- A thirty-nine year old teacher (female) belonging to Kottayam teaching at Kumarakom said: "For money, the children go to the tourism area and get abused. People at home should guide them and make them aware of the danger. If the children are properly cared and their simple needs satisfied, they wouldn't get into the vicious circle."
- Head Mistress of an aided school at Kumarakom said that while it was true that the children of that tourist spot were being corrupted, the parents were not concerned about what was happening to them. "The majority of the population of the locality are labourers.

They think that if they provide food and shelter to their children, their duty is over. The school going children are given packed food before eight o'clock in the morning by their mothers. They then go to work. They think that their childen will be okay at school and are unaware of what really happens." Yet, she added, "these children are not crooked".

- A forty-three year old male belonging to Chavara in Kollam district said: "There is nothing wrong in children using the mobile phones or internet. Yet they have to be aware of the widening 'deceit' on the net and mobile phone."
- Forty-nine-year-old female Higher Secondary School teacher belonging to Kollam said: "The children learn to be selfish at their home. They don't have a model parent at home who could guide them in the right direction. As for mobile phones and the net, the children are more attracted to the wrong use."
- Mr. Lalu Kumar, 47-year old, living at Kollam town of the same district said: "Drunken parents create disturbing atmosphere at home. At school, at least 20 per cent teachers lack proper perception, they are sadistic, and this fact is not brought into lime light."
- Reghunath, 49 years, belonging to Thrikkadavoor Panchayat, Kollam district: "The drive for money persuades the TV channels to conduct reality shows and film award nights that pollute the cultural heritage of the State. Those who are committed to the society are annoyed by what most of the TV channels do. The dress, the speech, the body language they project are indecent and impolite. The children who imitate this are mostly from families without a patriarch or matriarch to guide them. These children develop an attitude of apathy towards the society and do not hesitate to perform criminal acts. The school going children in Kollam town abscond from classes to wander about the Adventure Park, enter into sexual

abuse or drug dealing to make money. In the back waters of Alappuzha sex trade thrives. I predict that, unchecked, this would lead to terrible conditions of physical and mental health."

- Mr. Radhakrishnan, local secretary of a political party and newspaper agent at Kazhakkoottam, Thiruvananthapuram, said "In Elippakuzhy colony everything from small bomb making to child sex abuse happen. The adults work for mafia gangs. The children learn from them. The children consume opiates or alcohol and move around the beach. There is nothing that they can't do. At Kazhakkootam Govt. High School drug addiction and fight are usual. The school authorities over there have no voice."
- Head Mistress of Govt. High School, Kuttoor, Pathanamthitta district observed, "I have come to believe that alcoholism or addiction to alcohol is customary to the people of Kuttoor. At Govt. HS Kuttoor I have noticed at least twenty students who were under the impact of alcohol. Disciplinary action like expulsion is almost impossible because higher authorities tell us teachers that our job is to correct them and not punish them. I do not know ways to correct children belonging to the families with regular alcoholics. However, if the student teacher interaction improves and if teachers could really love the students, and if parents educate themselves to be model for children, remedy is possible."
- A forty-one year old primary school teacher from Kazhakkootam, Thiruvananthapuram district said that pressures of the circumstances have made the children of the day very selfish. She has noticed prolonged restlessness in many children in her classes. In her experience she has noticed children belonging to economically backward families becoming easy prey to objects of temptation like chooridars and mobile phones. She said that the child once out of home should feel

that "my parents love me and always wait for me at home. They always prey for my security. So I should return home without going wayward." She maintained that if the parents succeed in generating trust and love in the child's mind they wouldn't become prey to the perpetrators of abuse.

- A forty-nine year old graduate woman from Thiruvanantha-puram Corporation said "children tend to imitate their parents, their important looking neighbours, film stars and advertisement models. They are easily tempted into what others call folly. Parents and teachers should stop them from imitating wrong models."
- A fifty-year old woman, higher secondary schoolteacher, belonging to Pampady village in Kottayam district said: "Our state is a consumer state. Our people buy anything. Our children imitate this and long for everything. This at the very outset is the sign of an erroneous attitude to life. The source of the abuse you are worried about is the home itself. The parents either do not have time to play a role in the character building of their children or they are not aware of such a need. The appalling temper and the unethical behaviour of the father who is the head of the family explains the context of abuse. If someone can correct the father in the family everything would be smooth again."
- A forty-nine year old Ajitha Nair, Postgraduate, belonging to Changanacherry, Kottayam said, "The children do not get the attention they ought to have, at home or at school. Parents do not sincerely wish the children grow good, able individuals. Rather they are compelled to get hold of a rank in the examinations. When s/he goes down in the fight s/he becomes desperate and slips into the wrong trail where s/he is abused. It is found that the children are insulted in front of their classmates and friends. This will hurt his/her self-esteem. As for sexual abuse it is important that the

children are made aware of the traps ahead at crucial stages in their growth. However it is also important that appropriate punishments are given when they falter."

- A woman who did not disclose her age, who is perhaps in her forties, who the investigator met at Edappally in Ernakulam district said: "Nowadays in this region, there are only one or two children in any family. They are not brought up in a caring-sharing manner. The children are not children. In many walks of life they are more like adults. There are neither morals nor scruples in their life. They just want to catch every body's attention, for good or bad. And parents too don't care to listen to the woes of their children. The relationship is neither tender nor smooth. This is very sad."
- A forty-one year old male, teacher at Govt. Girls HS Manjeri, Malappuram district said, "The child of the day does not receive affection and a compassionate hearing to his complaints. At school the woman teachers far outnumber the males. Even some boys' schools are totally 'manned' by women. Due to many complex reasons these women are not able to effectively monitor and control the boys and girls with the result that these children learn more nonsense than sense at school. To ease this sorry state, a balanced number of committed male and female teachers who are well trained in student psychology should run the schools. This is a definite solution to child abuse in Kerala."
- A forty-seven year old woman belonging to Vengad in Kannur district said, "Parents seem to give a place to the children nowadays which the children of my days could not hope for. This has yet to help them. In the more complex and more selfish life of today, the parents put their children under pressure. Lack of knowledge of child psychology seems to be at the root. Balanced diet and a feeling of security will keep the children at least half way away from drugs and other forms of abuse."

- A student union leader said that private (unaided) schools in the State have become centres of physical, sexual and emotional abuse. Those in the cities are becoming breeding grounds of criminality. Adolescents who have a criminal background are active in the schools everywhere in Kerala and especially in the cities like Thiruvananthapuram and Kochi. Mushrooming of private schools, especially in the north of Kerala let sexuality and criminality flourish.
- Principal of NSS College, Cherthala, Alappuzha district, in a personal interview said that the UGC's grant for travel, etc., set to the students belonging to the backward rural communities (who include those below eighteen years and who are in the BPL category), on the very day of distribution is spent on liquor. Principal admitted that some parents along with a local toddy (palm wine) shopowner complained to him that the money goes waste on liquor. The owner of the toddy shop disclosed that on the eve of the fund distribution the recipient students consumed toddy worth rupees sixty thousand from his shop alone. The team appealed to the principal that in future, grants be distributed only in the presence of the concerned parent.

ANNEXURE II

An Extreme Instance of Child Abuse

Munchausen by proxy syndrome (MBPS) is one of the most harmful forms of child abuse and the most difficult to obtain evidence. In MBPS, an individual—usually a mother—deliberately makes her own preschool child sick or convinces others that the child is sick. Parent or care-giver misleads others into thinking that the child has medical problems by lying and reporting fictitious episodes. He or she may exaggerate, fabricate, or induce symptoms. As a result, doctors usually order tests, try different types of medications, and may even hospitalize the child or perform surgery to determine the cause. Because the parent or care-giver appears to be so caring and attentive, often no one suspects any wrongdoing. A perplexing aspect of the syndrome is the ability of the parent or care-giver to fool and manipulate doctors. Frequently, the perpetrator is familiar with the medical profession and is very good at fooling the doctors. Even the most experienced doctors can miss the meaning of the inconsistencies in the child's symptoms. It's not unusual for medical personnel to overlook the possibility of MBPS because it goes against the belief that a parent or care-giver would never deliberately hurt his or her child. Children who are subject to MBPS are typically preschool age, although there have been reported cases in kids up to 16 years old, and there are equal numbers of boys and girls. About 98 per cent of the perpetrators are female.

Indicators of MBPS

Diagnosis is very difficult, but would involve some of the following:

- A child who has multiple medical problems that do not respond to treatment or that follow a persistent and puzzling course.
- Physical or laboratory findings that are highly unusual, don't correspond with the child's medical history, or are physically or clinically impossible.
- Short-term symptoms that tend to stop when the perpetrator isn't around.

- A parent or care-giver who isn't reassured by "good news" when test results find no medical problems, but continues to believe that the child is ill.
- A parent or care-giver who appears to be medically knowledgeable or fascinated with medical details or appears to enjoy the hospital environment.
- A parent or care-giver who is unusually calm in the face of serious difficulties with the child's health.
- A parent or care-giver who's highly supportive and encouraging of the doctor, or one who is angry and demands further intervention, more procedures, second opinions, or transfers to more sophisticated facilities.

Causes of MBPS

In some cases, the parents or care-givers themselves were abused, both physically and sexually, as children. They may have come from families in which being sick was a way to get love. The parent's or care-giver's own personal needs overcome his or her ability to see the child as a person with feelings and rights, possibly because the parent or care-giver may have grown up being treated like he or she wasn't a person with rights or feelings.

What Happens to the Child?

In the most severe instances, parents or care-givers with MBPS may go to great lengths to make their children sick. When cameras were placed in some children's hospital rooms, some perpetrators were filmed switching medications, injecting kids with urine to cause an infection, or placing drops of blood in urine specimens.

Some perpetrators aggravate an existing problem, such as manipulating a wound so that it doesn't heal. One parent discovered that scrubbing the child's skin with oven cleaner would cause a baffling, long-lasting rash.

Whatever, the course, the child's symptoms—whether created or faked—don't happen when the parent isn't present, and they usually go away during periods of separation from the parent. When confronted, the parent usually denies knowing how the illness occurred.

According to experts, common conditions and symptoms that are created or faked by parents or care-givers with MBPS include—failure to thrive, allergies, asthma, vomiting, diarrhea, seizures, and infections.

The long-term prognosis for these children depends on the degree of damage created by the perpetrator and the amount of time it takes to recognize and diagnose MBPS. Some extreme cases have been reported in which children developed destructive skeletal changes, limps, mental retardation, brain damage, and blindness from symptoms caused by the parent or caregiver. Often, these children require multiple surgeries, each with the risk for future medical problems.

If the child lives to be old enough to comprehend what's happening, the psychological damage can be significant. The child may come to feel that he or she will only be loved when ill and may, therefore, help the parent try to deceive doctors, using self-abuse to avoid being abandoned. And so, some victims of MBPS later become perpetrators themselves. (*Source*: Internet)

References

Agarwal, Asok. 2011. Senior Advocate, Supreme Court, Interview in *Frontline*, Vol. 28, No. 14.

Albee George, W. 1980. "Primary Prevention and Social Problems". In George Gerbner, Edward Zigler *et al.* (Eds) *Child Abuse: An Agenda for Action*. Oxford: OUP, pp. 115-16.

An Intervention Study of Child Abuse in Kerala. 2005. Department of Social Welfare: Government of Kerala.

Aries, Philippe. 1962. *Centuries of Childhood: A Social History of Family Life*. New York: Vintage Publishers.

Bandura, A. 1973. *Aggression: A Social Learning Analysis*. New Jersey: Prentice Hall.

Basu, Kankana. 2010. "Childhood's End". In *The Hindu Magazine*, 7 Feb. (Weekly edition 2010).

"Be kind to these children." Editorial. *Mathrubhoomi* (Malayalam Daily). 20 March 2011.

Belsky, J. 1980. "Child Maltreatment: An Ecological Integration". *American Psychologist*. 35. 320:35.

Bhan, Susheela, C. Rajya Lakshmi. 1991. *Child Abuse: An Annotated Bibliography*. Delhi: Institute of Peace Research and Action.

Borocz, Jozsef. 2005. Redistributing Global Inequality. *Economic and Political Weekly*. 26 Feb. 886-92.

Bourne, R. and Newberger, E.H. (Eds). 1979. *Critical Perspectives on Child Abuse*. Lexington: Lexington Books.

Burgess, R.L. 1979. "Child Abuse: A Societal Interactional Analysis". In B.B. Lohey and A.E. Kazdin (Eds) *Advances in Clinical Child Psychology*, Vol. 2., 141–72. New York: Plenum Press.

Caffey, J. 1972. "On the theory and practice of shaking infants: Its potential residual effects of permanent brain damage and mental retardation". In *American Journal of Diseases of Children*, 124, 161-68.

Cantwell, A.B. 1980. 'Child Neglect'. In Kempe and R.E. Helfer (Eds) *The Battered Child*. Chicago: The University of Chicago Press.

Cohn Ruth, C. 2010. "The Issues in Values". In Mary Anne Kuebel, (Ed) *Living Learning*. Kottayam: RFC Interventions.

Debbie, Ariyo. *Africans Unite Against Child Abuse*. www.abusemuststop.org

Ezhuthachan, K.N. 1992. *Keralodaya*. Trivandrum: Department of Culture.

Gafoor, Abdul K.A. 2010. "Human Rights: Right to Life". In *Ragagiri Journal of Scoial Sciences*. Kalamassery: Rajagiri College of Social Sciences.

Garbarino, J. 1977. "The Human Ecology of Child Maltreatment". *Journal of Marriage and the Family*. 39(4), 721-35.

Garbarino, J. and Gilliam, G. 1980. *Understanding Abusive Families*, Massachussets: Lexington Books.

Gerbner, George. 1980. "Children and Power on Television: The Other Side of the Picture". In *Gerbner and Zigler*.

Gil, D. 1970. *Violence Against Children: Physical Abuse in the United States*. Cambridge: Harward University Press.

Gil, D.G. 1975. "Unravelling Child Abuse". *American Journal of Orthopsychiatry*, 45, 345-56.

Goode, William. 1971. "Force and Violence in the Family." *Journal of Marriage and the Family*. 33, 624-36.

Government of Canada.1984. "Sexual offences against children: Report of the Committee on Sexual Offences against children and youths". Ottawa: Ministry of Justice.

Hopper, Jim. 2009. In www.jimhopper.com

Johnson, C.F. 1985. "Injury Variable in Child Abuse". In *Child Abuse and Neglect*, 9, 207-15.

Karen, J. Swift. 1997. Canada: "Trends and Issues in Child Welfare". In Neil Gilbert (Ed) *Combating Child Abuse*. OUP: Oxford.

Kathleen, Gough E. 1993. "The Nayars and the Definition of Marriage". In Patricia Oberoi (Ed) *Family, Kinship and Marriage*. Delhi: OUP.

Kempe, C.H. *et al.* 1962. "The Battered Child Syndrome". *Journal of the American Medical Association.* 181(1), 17-24.

"Kerala Child Abuse: An assessment of the current situation", Editorial, *Mathrubhoomi*, 6 July 2011.

Kessler, Marc and Albee, George, W. 1975. Primary Prevention. *Annual Review of Psychology*. California: Annual Reviews Press.

Korbin, J. 1981. *Child Abuse and Neglect: Cross Cultural Perspectives*. Berkeley: University of California Press.

Kunjan, Pillai, Elamkulam. 1970. *Studies in Kerala History*. Kottayam: National Book Stall.

Lawrence, Ruth. 1997. "United States: California's Reporting System". In Neil Gilbert (Ed) *Combating Child Abuse*. (Ed) OUP: Oxford.

Madhavan, T.K. 1954. "The more the path changes". In P.K. Balakrishnan (Ed) *Sreenarayanaguru*. Kottayam: D.C. Books.

Masson, J. 1984. *Freud: The Assault on Truth*. London: Faber and Faber.

Mateer, Samuel. 1883. *Native Life in Travancore*. London: W.H. Allen and Co.

Mateer, Samuel. 1870. *The Land of Charity: A Descriptive Account of Travancore and its People*. London: John Snow and Co.

Menon Sreedhara, A. 2007(rpt). *A Survey of Kerala History*. Kottayam: DC Books.

Ministry of Women and Child Development. 2007. *Study on Child Abuse: India 2007*. New Delhi: Government of India.

Padmanabhan, Mannathu. 1998. *The Reminiscences of My Life*. Trivandrum: Cultural Publications Department, Government of Kerala.

Pallath, J.J. 2004. "Social Stigma and Identity Crisis of MSM/ Gay in Kerala". Kannur: Jeevana Samskriti (Unpublished Project Report submitted to SMA/KSACS).

Panikkar, K.N. 2011. "Culture and Making of a Nation". *Frontline*. Vol. 28, No. 14.

Parton, N. 1989. 'Child abuse'. In B. Kahan (Ed) *Child Care Research, Policy and Practice*. London: Hodder and Stoughton.

Pecora, P.J. *et al.* 1992. *The Child Welfare Challenge: Policy, Practice, and Research*. New York: Aldine de Gruyter.

Peters, R.T. 2008. "Justice in a World Gone Mad: Assessing the Ethical Landscape of Globalization". In Ronald Commers *et al.* (Eds) *Ethics in An Era of Globalization*. Hampshire: Ashgate.

Ramakrishnan, Mathangi. 2010. "Dimensions of Child Maltreatment". In *The Hindu* 21 April 2010.

Ryan, Chris and Michael Hall, C. 2001. *Sex Tourism: Marginal People and Liminalities*. London and New York: Routledge.

Sadgopal, Anil. 2011. Neoliberal Act: *Frontline*. Vol. 28, No. 14. 4-5.

Schene, P. 1987. "Is Child Abuse Decreasing"? In *Journal of Interpersonal Violence*, 2(2): 225-27.

Segal, Uma A. 1996. "Children as Witnesses: India is not Ready". In Betty, L. Bottoms (Ed) *International Perspectives on Child Abuse and Child Testimony*. California: Sage Publications.

Sen, Amartya K. 1999. *Development as Freedom*. New York: Knopf.

Showers, J., Bardman, R.L. 1988. Scarring for Life: Abuse with electric cords. *Child Abuse and Neglect*. 10, 25-31.

Singh, Ram Sankar. 2009. *Encyclopaedia on Women and Children Trafficking*, Vol. 1. New Delhi: Anmol Publications.

Slovan, I.J. 1983. *Child Abuse: Law and Legislation*. New York: Oceana Publications.

Spinetta, J.J. 1972. "The Child Abusing Parent: A Psychological Review". In *Psychological Bulletin*, 77: 296-304.

Tarja, Poso. 1997. "Finland: Child Abuse as Family Problem". In Neil Gilbert (Ed) *Combating Child Abuse: International Perspectives and Trends*. New York: OUP.

Tulir. 2011. *Myths and Facts*. <tulircphcsa.org>

U.K. Department of Health, 1989. *An Introduction to the Children Act 1989*. London: Her Majesty's Stationery Office.

U.K. Home Office, Department of Health, Department of Education and Science and Welsh Office. 1991. *Working Together Under the Children Act 1989*. London: Her Majesty's Stationery Office.

UNDP. 1998. *The State of Human Development, Human Development Report*. New York: United Nations Development Programme.

Wirani, Pinki. 2000. *Bitter Chocolate: Child Sexual Abuse in India*. New Delhi: Penguin Books.

Wise, J.M. 2008. *Cultural Globalization: A User's Guide*. Carlton: Blackwell Publishing.

Zelizer, V.A. 1985. *Pricing the Priceless Child: The Changing Social Value of Children*. New York: Basic Books.